OECD Proceedings

Valuing Rural Amenities

OECD

ORGANISATION FOR ECONOMIC CO-OPERATION AND DEVELOPMENT

ORGANISATION FOR ECONOMIC CO-OPERATION AND DEVELOPMENT

Pursuant to Article 1 of the Convention signed in Paris on 14th December 1960, and which came into force on 30th September 1961, the Organisation for Economic Co-operation and Development (OECD) shall promote policies designed:

- to achieve the highest sustainable economic growth and employment and a rising standard of living in Member countries, while maintaining financial stability, and thus to contribute to the development of the world economy;
- to contribute to sound economic expansion in Member as well as non-member countries in the process of economic development; and
- to contribute to the expansion of world trade on a multilateral, non-discriminatory basis in accordance with international obligations.

The original Member countries of the OECD are Austria, Belgium, Canada, Denmark, France, Germany, Greece, Iceland, Ireland, Italy, Luxembourg, the Netherlands, Norway, Portugal, Spain, Sweden, Switzerland, Turkey, the United Kingdom and the United States. The following countries became Members subsequently through accession at the dates indicated hereafter: Japan (28th April 1964), Finland (28th January 1969), Australia (7th June 1971), New Zealand (29th May 1973), Mexico (18th May 1994), the Czech Republic (21st December 1995), Hungary (7th May 1996), Poland (22nd November 1996) and Korea (12th December 1996). The Commission of the European Communities takes part in the work of the OECD (Article 13 of the OECD Convention).

Foreword

This two-day workshop (5-6 June 2000), hosted by the USDA and attended by around sixty representatives from OECD Agriculture, Rural Development and Environment ministries, focused on the contribution that natural and cultural amenities, including externalities and public goods from agriculture and ecological resources, make to the development of rural areas, and identified valuation methods and policy instruments that can help to promote this contribution. In particular, the workshop concentrated on two key areas: assessing the merits and limitations of 1) methods of estimating the demand for, and deriving the value of, non-market amenities, and 2) instruments to encourage the creation of market or market-type mechanisms to capture the non-marketed benefits of rural amenities, maintain and enhance supply, and correct potential costs to society in case of market failure. The workshop had the ultimate aim of assessing whether some set of international guidelines or standards could be used to reduce the subjectivity of the evidentiary information.

This workshop built on work undertaken by the OECD in three main areas – territorial development (rural policy), agriculture (multifunctionality and agri-environmental indicators) and environment (economic aspects of biodiversity).

The question of how to harness the potential of amenities for rural development has been, for several years, a principal component of the work programme of the OECD's Territorial Development Service (TDS) on rural policy. This workshop will help to connect the conceptual and case study work completed by TDS on rural amenities (published as *Cultivating Rural Amenities: An Economic Development Perspective* – OECD, 1999), with more in-depth policy analysis to be launched in 2000. The workshop also extends valuation-related work undertaken by the OECD's Environment and Agriculture directorates, notably in a seminar entitled *Benefit Valuation of Biodiversity Resources* organised by the OECD's Working Group on Economic Aspects of Biodiversity in October 1999, and contributions to the OECD project on agri-environmental indicators, in particular, the publication *Environmental Indicators for Agriculture*, Vol. 3; *Methods and Results* (OECD, January 2001). The outcomes from the workshop will feed into ongoing work in these two fields. The workshop will also constitute an important input to debate at the OECD on the multifunctional character of agriculture, and ongoing work on agri-environmental policies.

Table of Contents

List of Tables

List of Figures

List of Boxes

Chapter 1

Introduction

by
Douglas Macmillan
Department of Agriculture, University of Aberdeen

Methods for valuing non-market environmental benefits have been under development for many years. Early work in the 1960s and 1970s focused on recreational activities such as hunting and hiking, and later on environmental pollution. More recently, rural amenity valuation has attracted considerable attention from economists, particularly in Europe where considerable policy emphasis is placed on the social, environmental and cultural benefits of agriculture.

Valuation research in the area of rural amenities is now global and plays an increasingly important role in policy formulation and implementation in many countries. The overall aim of the workshop was to examine the contribution economic valuation methods and economic policy instruments can make to the provision of rural amenity benefits from agriculture and other ecological resources.

The workshop was divided into two main sessions. On the first day, methods for assessing demand and deriving value for rural amenities were discussed, with papers from Ståle Navrud (Agricultural University of Norway), Jose Lima e Santos (Technical University of Lisbon) and John Foster (University of Lancaster). Discussions on the second day centred on the supply side, and the design of suitable policies for transforming values into revenues, with papers from Ian Hodge (University of Cambridge) and Ralph Heimlich (ERS-USDA). The concluding paper was presented by David Baldock, Director of the Institute for European Environmental Policy, and gave an overview of the wider policy implications of the issues surrounding valuing rural amenities.

The meeting was introduced by Professor Kerry Smith of North Carolina State University, who outlined the state of the art with regard to valuation methods, and some of the current issues in the debate about valuation and rural policy. These issues, concerning reliability, general equilibrium effects, benefit transfer, and the role of monetary benefit estimates in policy development were subsequently developed in the main workshop papers.

Ståle Navrud provides a brief review of monetary and non-monetary valuation techniques and describes their limitations and advantages for policy-making. He suggests that while methods such as multi-criteria analysis which rely on expert opinion, together with other criteria (*e.g.*, equity considerations, political accept-ability) have an important role to play, monetary valuation is still necessary if deci-sions are to remain relevant to economic efficiency.

The advantages and disadvantages of benefit transfer are also presented. Ben-efit transfer is the term given to methods for transferring benefit estimates from one geographical area and context to another area and context. Benefit transfer, although simple in principal, faces problems with data availability, and dealing with differences between the sites and populations of interest. Thus far in its develop-ment, benefit transfer has not achieved any significant degree of reliability and suffers, perhaps a little prematurely, from the reputation of being a rather "quick and dirty" solution. However, as Navrud suggests, more investment in research is certainly worthwhile because the rewards to policy development, in terms of avoiding the need for new valuation studies and more reliable decision-making, are considerable.

Professor Santos also touches on some of the problems of benefit transfer with his paper on the problems and potential of valuing multiple outputs from agricul-ture. Rural land activities such as agriculture and forestry can generate a whole range of non-market outputs including landscape, biodiversity, recreation and cul-tural tradition. Santos proves from a theoretical analysis, that policy benefits can be over-estimated if individual outputs are valued separately and then added together in a benefit transfer exercise, for example. This effect can be best explained in terms of substitution and income effects among consumers. Although corrections can be made to account for this error, the best solution is to value rural amenities as a package, rather than as separate components of a given policy.

John Foster, a psychologist from Lancaster University, takes a rather more scep-tical view of valuation in policy development and instrument design. He questions the validity and moral legitimacy of valuing the environment in monetary terms and gives examples of projects, such as the site for the third London Airport, where val-uation and Cost-Benefit Analysis was controversial, and perhaps hindered rather than helped the decision-making process. Valuation, he argues, is too simplistic and artificial to capture the richness and complexity of environmental decisions and may be leading officials to assume a greater degree of public accord with their approaches than may in fact exist.

Foster concludes by suggesting that a fresh approach to environmental deci-sion-making may well be needed. Citizen juries and other discussion fora, which allow a more open expression and interchange of views than existing survey-based techniques such as Contingent Valuation, are a much richer source of information for the policy maker. As many economists share these doubts about the suitability of survey approaches to valuation, (after all who ever purchases anything via a survey?), there is perhaps a need to introduce more discussion-based approaches to valuation exercises.

The second session of the workshop was devoted to the question of transforming values into revenues through appropriate policy responses, with papers from Ian Hodge and Ralph Heimlich. The rationale, strengths and weaknesses of current policy instruments were outlined by Hodge. He argues that diversity in the characteristics of rural amenities, and the importance of the local historical, environmental and social context of these amenities require that a complex mix of private and public delivery mechanisms are developed. An interesting distinction is made here between "Old" and "New World" approaches to policy. Looking forward, the main challenges will be problems with measurement and valuation, sensitivity to local context, and achieving collective action where supply is influenced by spatial location.

Heimlich provides a detailed account of experience in the United States with a range of voluntary incentive programmes for rural amenities, including the Conservation Reserve Program and US wetland policy. The paper discusses the rationale for incentive programmes and the influence, or rather the lack of influence, valuation studies have had thus far on the design and implementation of policy. Valuation studies have not been directly part of programme implementation due to resource constraints, although it has had a role in helping scope programs and bringing out what is to be gained or lost as a result. Cost-effectiveness is widely regarded as a more practicable tool for ex-post appraisal as it is more easily grasped and understood by program officials, and can deal with the often messy multiple objective character of real programs as well.

The concluding paper for the workshop reminds us that the term rural amenities encompasses perhaps a wider group of issues than reflected in the preceding papers, and covers emerging issues about environmental ethics and farm animal welfare. Baldock reviews the potential role of valuation in the international arena level, and describes the beginnings of an intersection between the rural amenity valuation debate and the well-established and on-going discussions about international trade. The crux of this debate, which is reflected in the Workshop papers and in the Round Table discussions, is whether rural amenity values are a credible and reliable basis for guiding the evolution of policy support for farmers. This debate has only just begun, and it is hoped that the papers presented in this volume will help to inform and encourage further discussions by policy-makers and academics alike.

Part 1
ASSESSING DEMAND AND DERIVING VALUE

Chapter 2

Valuation Techniques and Benefit Transfer Methods: Strengths, Weaknesses and Policy Utility

by
Ståle Navrud
Department of Economics and Social Sciences,
Agricultural University of Norway

1. Whose preferences should count?

Economists have developed a variety of techniques to value non-market environmental and cultural amenities consistent with the valuation of marketed goods; *i.e.*, based on individual preferences. These techniques are based upon either observed behaviour (revealed preferences; RP) towards some marketed good with a connection to the non-marketed good of interest, or stated preferences (SP) in surveys with respect to the non-marketed good; see Table 1, Part I for an overview of these techniques. While RP and SP techniques are based on individual preferences, and are rooted in welfare economics, other methods for economic valuation of environmental and cultural amenities have also been proposed. These methods are based on the preferences of policy makers, scientific experts or specific interest groups. I will first review some of these techniques, before focusing on methods based on individual preferences, which is the basis for most policy uses of environmental valuation techniques, including cost-benefit analysis (CBA) and externality adders/environmental costing.

Table 1, Part II gives an overview of these alternative techniques to environmental valuation. The method of Implicit Valuation (IV) derives values that are implicit in policy decisions. IV assumes that the policy makers had complete information about the impacts on the environmental goods, and that we are able to sort out these values from other considerations implicit in the decision; see Carlsen *et al.* (1994) for an empirical application of the IV technique. This technique can be viewed as an indirect, revealed preference method, but reveal policy makers' preferences rather than individual preferences. (Democratically elected policy makers

Table 1. **Classification of environmental valuation techniques**

	Indirect	Direct
	I. Methods based on individual preferences	

Revealed Preferences (RP)	Household Production Function (HPF) Approach:
	  Travel Cost (TC) method
	  Averting Costs (AC)
	Hedonic Price (HP) analysis
		Simulated markets
		Market prices
		Replacement Costs (RC)

Stated Preferences (SP)	Contingent Ranking (CR) Choice Experiments (CE): Conjoint Analysis	Contingent Valuation (CV)
	II. Methods based on decision-makers'/experts'/interest groups' preferences	
Revealed Preferences (RP) Stated Preferences (SP)	Implicit Valuation (IV) Delphi Method	Multi Criteria Analysis (MCA)

could be said to represent individual preferences, but policy makers might pursue own interests that could conflict with individual preferences). In spite of the potential biases of IV, the method could serve as a corrective to policy makers by making them aware of the economic values they implicitly assign to environmental and cultural goods through the decisions they have made. The method can also be used to make policy makers aware of implicit values from decisions they are about to make, e.g., by pointing out the values they would implicitly attach to unvalued environmental impacts in a CBA dependent upon the project alternative they choose.

Delphi methods can be used to solicit the opinions of experts. Most Delphi exercises administer one or more questionnaires interspersed with information to a group of experts. Typically, the experts are polled one or more times; and between pollings, information about the opinions of the group of experts as a whole is disseminated among the group (Ziglio, 1996). In the case of valuing environmental goods and environmental related health impacts, the experts could be natural scientists and health experts as in Navrud (1997), or environmental economists as in Carson et al. (1997). Carson et al. (1997) asked a panel of 30 European environmental economists familiar with contingent valuation (CV) to estimate the economic value of a global public good; the Fes Medina in Morocco (which was put on the UNESCO World Cultural and Natural Heritage list as early as 1980). In this case the experts were asked not about their own opinion concerning the value of the restoration of the Fes Medina, but rather for their professional judgements as to what they would expect the estimate of the non-market economic value to be in their respective countries and in Europe as a whole if a contingent valuation (CV) study concerning restoration of Fes Medina were to be considered. Thus, in this case experts provide one number representing public value for a given good when the value is measured in a certain way, making the results verifiable in principle. (This exercise can be viewed as each respondent performing a simple value transfer exercise in the first phase, but then in the second phase, which is typical of a Delphi exercise, they are asked whether they will reconsider their values having seen the results the others gave.) This sort of Delphi study can be viewed as indirectly reflecting individual preferences, since experts are not asked about their own preferences, but to predict individual preferences.

Multi Criteria Analysis (MCA) involves identifying decision criteria (one of which could be a monetary measure), a scale for each criteria and different alternatives that scores differently for the different criteria. Then, the experts are asked to choose between the alternatives. A software packages is used to calculate the implicit weights for each criteria (which their choices imply), the scores for each criteria of the different alternatives are changed, and the experts are asked to make a new choices. After a number of iterations, a set of criteria weights can be calculated. This is only one approach of weighting and scoring under MCA. It is also possible to calculate the implicit tradeoffs between units of each criterion in terms of the units of a specified criterion. If, for example, the cost of alternative measures to preserve the agricultural landscape is one of the criteria, this procedure can be used to calculate the willingness-to-pay for changes in the aesthetic beauty of agricultural landscape (assuming that marginal changes in this environmental good could be identified and measured in a meaningful way). This specific MCA technique has much in common with the indirect stated preference methods known as choice experiments (CE), but elicit preferences of decision makers, experts or interest groups rather than the preferences of a random sample of the affected individuals.

Wenstøp and Carlsen (1998) used a scenario description of environmental impacts from a hydroelectric development project, which had previously been used in a contingent valuation (CV) study of a random sample of the local population (Navrud, 1994), in their MCA. They found a mean WTP to avoid the negative impacts on recreation, ecosystems and cultural heritage among their three panels of representatives from the departments and agencies of environment and energy, the developer and a local politician, to be 14 per cent lower than the aggregated individual WTP in the CV study. Thus, in this specific study the difference between individual preferences and the preferences of interest groups/decision makers was small. However, there is no reason to expect that this will always be the case, and the basic question becomes: Whose preferences should count?

Welfare economics and its applied tool, CBA, are based on individual preferences, and will ensure that these preferences are taken into account when decisions are made. Experiences from both Europe and USA (Navrud and Pruckner, 1997) have shown that CBA and other uses for environmental valuation techniques are used as an input in environmental decision-making, but not as a stand-alone decision- making device. Even though cost effectiveness plays a major role in establishing environmental programmes, the decision-maker also considers other criteria (*e.g.*, equity considerations, administrative cost, and "political acceptability"). However, to be consistent with the basic welfare economic principles underlying CBA, environmental valuation techniques based on individual preferences should be used. Techniques based on preferences of decision-makers, interest groups or experts can be used as an alternative or complementary decision tool to CBA.

2. Valuation techniques based on individual preferences

Revealed Preference techniques can be divided into direct and indirect methods. Direct methods include **simulated market exercises** (*i.e.*, constructing a real market for a public good). This is most often not possible to do, and when possible, it s usually very time-consuming and costly. Some environmental impacts can be valued using dose-response functions and **market prices,** *e.g.*, impacts on crops, forests and building materials (corrosion and soiling) from air pollution. This approach uses only the physical or biological dose-response relationship to estimate the response to a change in some environmental parameter. The observed market price of the activity or entity is then multiplied by the magnitude of the physical or biological response to obtain a monetary measure of damage. Thus, neither behavioural adaptations nor price responses are taken into account. Simple multiplication provides an accurate estimate of economic behaviour and value – in this case changes in gross revenue – only if economic agents are limited in the ways in which they can adapt to the environmental effect and if the effect is small enough to have little or no impact on relative prices. This combination of circumstances is very unlikely. If *e.g.*, crop damages from air pollution is large enough to change prices, changes in consumer and producer surpluses have to be calculated. If farmers undertake preventive measures, *e.g.*, switching to crops that are less sensitive to air pollution, the simple multiplication approach will overestimate damage costs. Thus, other approaches should be use, see Adams and Crocker (1991).

The **replacement cost method** (also termed restoration cost method) has been used to estimate economic damages from soil erosion, by using market prices for soil and fertilisers to calculate what it would cost to replace the lost soils. This approach has also been used to calculate loss of ecosystem functions. Restoration costs are, however, just arbitrary values that might bear little relationship to true social values. Individuals "willingness-to-pay" (WTP) for the restoration of environmental and cultural amenities may be more or less than the cost of replacement.

The greatest advantages of these direct RP methods are that they are relatively simple to use. But as noted earlier, the methods ignore the behavioural responses of individuals to changes in the environmental amenities. They also obscure the distinction between benefits and costs – there is no guarantee that people are actually willing to pay the estimated cost.

The indirect RP methods entail two main groups of methods; the household production function approach (including the popular Travel Cost method and Averting Cost method; and the hedonic price analysis).

The **household production function** (HPF) approach involves investigating changes in consumption of commodities that are substitutes or complements for the environmental attribute. The *Travel Cost* (TC) method, used widely to measure the demand for recreation, is a prominent example. The costs of travelling to a recreation site together with participation rates, visitor attributes, and information about substitute sites are used to derive a measure for the use value of the recreational activity at the site. Travel can be used to infer the demand for recreation, only if it is a necessary part of the visit, or in economic terms is a *weak complement*. TC models builds on a set of strict assumptions, which are seldom fulfilled, and the results are sensitive to the specification of the TC model, the choice of functional forms, treatment of travel time and substitute sites, etc. However, they can be relatively cheap to perform (compared to SP methods), and give reasonably reliable estimates for *use* values of natural resources (*e.g.*, recreational fishing, hunting and hiking) for the *current* quality off a site.

Another example of the use of the household production function approach is the use of *Averting Costs* (AC) (also known as defensive or preventive expenditures) to infer value. Averting inputs include air filters, water purifiers, noise insulation, and other means of mitigating personal impacts of pollution. Such inputs substitute for changes in environmental attributes; in effect the quality of a consumer's personal environment is a function of the quality of the collective environment and the use of averting inputs. We measure the value of changes in the collective environment by examining costs incurred in using averting inputs to make the personal environment different from the collective environment. A rational consumer will buy averting inputs to the point where the marginal rate of substitution between purchased inputs and the collective environment equals the price ratio. By characterising the rate of substitution and knowing the price paid for the substitute, we can infer the price that consumers would be willing to pay for a change in the environment. The common element in household production methods is the use of changes in the *quantities* of complements to estimate the value of a change in quality.

The household production function (HPF) method uses actual behaviour as the basis for valuation, but is limited to *use value*. Non-use values, that do not entail direct consumption, cannot be estimated by looking at complements or substitutes. HPF approaches have mostly been used to value recreational activities, health and material damages.

Hedonic Price (HP) analysis refers to the estimation of implicit prices for individual attributes of a market commodity. Some environmental goods and services can be viewed as attributes of a market commodity, such as real property. For example, proximity to noisy streets, noisy airports and polluted waterways; odours from hog operations, factories, sewage treatment plants and waste disposal sites; exposure to polluted air, and access to parks or scenic vistas are purchased along with residential property. Part of the variation in property prices is due to differences in these amenities. Other applications have been to wages for jobs that entail different levels of physical risks (termed hedonic wage models), mortality valuation to estimate the Value of a Statistical Life (VSL). HP data can be quite costly to get, as there is often no database of residential properties which has data on all attributes, including environmental amenities that could affect property prices. In addition, the second stage of the HP analysis is often impossible to do since we lack socio-economic data on the buyers of residential properties. The HP function is very sensitive to the specification and functional form, and it is often difficult to find a measure for the environmental amenity where data exist, and for which the bidders for residential properties can recognise marginal changes in and have complete information about at the time they bid for the property. Two examples: i) There is often no data on traffic noise levels, but using the annual average number of vehicles on the nearest road or distance to this road as proxy variables for noise levels, could easily value all road traffic related externalities (including accident risks, health impacts from air pollution, barrier effects and soiling); ii) Properties are shown to potential buyers on Sundays when there is little traffic on the nearby road, and thus they place their bid on the property with incomplete information about the road traffic noise level.

While (indirect) RP methods are based on actual behaviour in a market for goods related to the environmental good in question (and thus the value for the environmental goods is elicited based on sets of strict assumptions about this relationship), SP methods measure the value of the environmental good in question by constructing a hypothetical market for the good. The hypothetical nature is the main argument against SP methods. However, no strict assumptions about the relationship between marketed complements or substitutes, or attributes of a marketed good and the environmental good have to be made. SP methods also have the advantages of being able to measure the Total Economic Value (TEV), including both use and non-use value (also termed passive use value), derives the "correct" Hicksian welfare measure, and can measure *future changes* in environmental quality.

The Stated Preference methods can be divided into direct and indirect approaches. The direct Contingent Valuation (CV) method is by far the most used method, but over the past few years the indirect approaches of Contingent Ranking (CR) and Choice Experiments (CE) have gained popularity. The main difference between these two approaches is that while the CV method typically is a two-alternative (referendum) approach, CE employs a series of questions with more than two alternatives that are designed to elicit responses allowing for estimation of preferences over attributes of an environmental state.

A **Contingent Valuation (CV)** survey constructs scenarios that offer different possible future government actions. Under the simplest and most commonly used CV question format, the respondent is offered a binary choice between two alternatives, one being the status quo policy, the other alternative policy having a cost greater than maintaining the status quo. The respondent is told that the government will impose the stated cost (*e.g.*, increased taxes, higher prices associated with regulation, or user fees) if the non status quo alternative is provided. The key elements here are that the respondent provides a "favour/not favour answer" with respect to the alternative policy (versus the status quo), what the alternative policy will provide, how it will be provided, and how much it will cost, and how it will be charged for (*i.e.*, payment vehicle), have been clearly specified. This way of eliciting willingness-to-pay is termed binary *discrete choice*. An alternative elicitation method is *open-ended* questions where respondents are asked directly about the most they would be willing to pay to get the alternative policy (with or without the visual aid of a payment card, *i.e.*, randomly chosen amounts ranging from zero to some expected upper amount). One of the main challenges in a CV study is to describe the change in the environmental or cultural amenity the alternative policy will provide in a way that is understandable to the respondent and at the same time scientifically correct.

Concerns raised by CV critics over the reliability of the CV approach led the US National Oceanic and Atmospheric Administration (NOAA) to convene a panel of eminent experts co-chaired by Nobel Prize winners Kenneth Arrow and Robert Solow to examine the issue. In January 1993, the Panel, after lengthy public hearing and reviewing many written submissions, issued a report which concluded that "CV *studies can produce estimates reliable enough to be the starting point for a judicial or administrative determination of natural resources damages – including lost passive use value"* (Arrow *et al.*, 1993). The Panel suggested guidelines for use in Natural Resource Damage Assessment (NRDA) legal cases to help ensure the reliability of CV surveys on passive use values including the use of in-person interviews, a binary discrete choice question, a careful description of the good and its substitutes, and several different tests should be included in the report on survey results. Since the Panel has issued the report, many empirical tests have been conducted and several key theoretical issues have been clarified. The simplest test corresponds to a well-known economic maxim, the higher the cost the lower the demand. This price sensitivity test can easily be tested in the binary discrete choice format, by observing whether the percentage favouring the project falls as the randomly assigned cost of the project increases, which rarely fails in empirical applications. The test that has attracted the most attention in recent years is whether WTP estimates from CV studies increase in a plausible manner with the quantity or scope of the good being provided. CV critics often argue that insensitivity to scope results from what they term "warm-glow", by which they mean getting moral satisfaction from the act

21

of paying for the good independent of the characteristics of the actual environmental good. There have now been a considerable number of tests of the scope insensitivity hypothesis (also termed "embedding"), and recent review of the empirical evidence suggests that the hypothesis is rejected in a large majority of the tests performed (Carson, 1997).

Producing a good CV survey instrument requires substantial development work; typically including focus groups, in-depth interviews, pre-test and pilot studies to help determine plausibility and understandability of the good and scenario being presented. The task of translating technical material into a form understood by the general public is often a difficult one. Adding to the high costs of CV surveys is the recommended mode of survey administration being in-person interviews (Arrow et al., 1993). Mail and telephone surveys are dramatically cheaper, but mail surveys suffer from sample selection bias (i.e., those returning the survey are typically more interested in the issue than those who do not) and phone surveys have severe drawbacks if the good is complicated or visual aids are needed. CV results can be quite sensitive to the treatment of potential outliers. Open-ended survey questions typically elicit a large number of so-called protest zeros and a small number of extremely high responses. In discrete choice CV questions, econometric modelling assumptions can often have a substantial influence on results obtained. Any careful analysis will involve a series of judgmental decisions about how to handle specific issues involving the data, and these decisions should be clearly noted.

According to Carson (2000) the recent debate surrounding the use of CV is, to some degree, simply a reflection of the large sums at stake in major environmental decisions involving passive use and the general distrust that some economists have for information collected from surveys. Outside of academic journals, criticism of CV has taken a largely anecdotal form, ridiculing the results of particular CV studies, many of which use techniques known to be problematic. The implication drawn is that all CV surveys produce nonsense results upon which no reasonable person would rely. In an academic context, however, the debate over the use of CV has been more productive. The spotlight placed upon CV has matured it; its theoretical foundations and limits to its users are now better understood. The CV method has still not reached the routine application stage, and all CV surveys should include new research/tests. Carson (2000) concludes that perhaps the most pressing need is on how to reduce the costs of CV surveys while still maintaining a high degree of reliability, and suggests combination telephone-mail-telephone surveys to reduce survey administration costs and implementation of research programs designed at solving some of the more generic representation issues such as low level risk and large scale ecosystems.

Choice experiments (CEs) have been employed in marketing, transportation and psychology literature for some time, and arose from conjoint analysis, which is commonly used in marketing and transportation research. CEs differ from typical conjoint methods in that individuals are asked to choose from alternative bundles of attributes instead of ranking or rating them. Under the CE approach respondents are asked to pick their most favoured out of a set of three or more alternatives, and are typically given multiple sets of choice questions. Because CEs are based on attributes, they allow the researcher to value attributes as well as situational changes. Furthermore, in the case of damage to a particular attribute, compensating amounts of other goods (rather than compensation based on money) can be calculated. This is one of the approaches that can be used in Natural Resource Damage Assessments (NRDAs). An attribute-based approach is necessary to measure the type or amount of other "goods" that are required for compensation (Adamowicz *et al.*, 1998). This approach can provide substantially more information about a range of possible alternative policies as well as reduce the sample size needed compared to Contingent Valuation (CV). However, survey design issues with the CE approach are often much more complex due to the number of goods that must be described and the statistical methods that must be employed. Another drawback is that they provide incentives for strategic behaviour on the part of survey respondents (*i.e.*, CE is not incentive compatible). Carson *et al.* (1999) provides the following example: Consider the case of air pollution levels in a city. The agent (respondent) is asked to choose between different pairs of air pollution levels that involve different costs and different health effects and visibility levels. Any particular method that the agent perceives that the agency is using to incorporate agent preferences into its choice of an air pollution level, which all agents will face since this is a public good, generally provides incentives for non-truthful preference revelation. In some instances it will even be optimal for the agent to reject his or her most preferred level in a particular paired comparison. Once this is possible, the standard methods of inferring value from choice no longer work. CV questions, however, using binary discrete choice questions for new public goods with coercive payment (not voluntary payments), choices between which of two new public goods to provide, and changes in an existing private or quasi-private good (not introduction of new private or quasi-public goods) are incentive compatible.

Both types of SP methods have been successfully applied to value agricultural landscape, see *e.g.*, Dubgaard *et al.* (1994), Pruckner (1995) and Santos (1998).

3. Use of valuation techniques in policy

Environmental valuation studies have four main types of use (Navrud and Pruckner, 1997):

1. Cost-benefit analysis (CBA) of investment projects and policies.

2. Environmental costing in order to map the marginal environmental and health damages of *e.g.*, air, water and soil pollution from energy production, waste treatment and other production and consumption activities. These

23

marginal external cost can be used in investment decisions and operation (*e.g.*, as the basis for "green taxes").

3. Environmental accounting at the national level (green national accounts), local level (community green accounts) and firm level (environmental reporting). And

4. Natural Resource Damage Assessment (NRDA); *i.e.*, compensation payments for natural resource injuries from *e.g.*, pollution accidents.

Environmental valuation techniques have mostly been used in CBAs, but are now increasingly used also in NDRAs in the US; environmental costing of electricity production from different energy sources in both the US and Europe (see *e.g.*, Rowe *et al.*, 1995; Desvousges *et al.*, 1998; and European Commission–DG XII, 1995 and 1999); and green national accounting exercises, *e.g.*, the Green Accounting Research Project (GARP) of the European Commission (Tamborra, 1999; GARP II, 1999). The accuracy needed increases, and thus the applicability of benefit transfer techniques decreases, as we move down the list of potential policy uses of valuation studies (Navrud and Pruckner, 1997).

CBA has a long tradition in the US as a project evaluation tool, and has also been used extensively as an input in decision making ever since President Reagan issued Executive Order (EO) 12292 in 1981, necessitating a formal analysis of costs and benefits for federal environmental regulations that impose significant costs or economic impacts (*i.e.*, Regulatory Impact Analysis). In Europe, CBA has a long tradition in evaluation of transportation investment projects in many countries, but environmental valuation techniques were in most cases not applied. There seems to be no legal basis for CBA in any European country, but the UK Environment Act requires a comparison of costs and benefits. Some countries have administrative CBA guidelines for project and policy evaluation, and in a few cases these include a section on environmental valuation techniques.

Paragraph 130r of the Maastricht Treaty, which focuses on EU's environmental goals, environmental protection measures and international co-operation in general, says that the EU will consider the burden and advantage of environmental action or non-action. Furthermore, the "Fifth Activity Programme for Environmental Protection Towards Sustainability" (1993-2000) says: *"In accordance with the Treaty, an analysis of the potential costs and benefits of action and non-action will be undertaken in developing specific formal proposals within the Commission. In developing such proposals every care will be taken as far as possible to avoid the imposition of disproportionate costs and to ensure that the benefits will outweigh the costs over time"* (European Community, 1993, p. 142). The 1994 Communication from the Commission to the Council of the European Parliament, entitled: "Directions for the EU on Environmental Indicators and Green National accounting – The Integration of Environmental and Economic Information Systems" [COM(94)670, final 21.12.94] states a specific action for *"improving the methodology and enlarging the scope for monetary valuation of environmental damage"*. More recently, the EC's Green Paper, entitled "For a European Union Energy Policy", states that *"internalisation of external costs is central to energy and environmental policy"*. During the last few years the European Commission has performed CBAs of two new regulations; the large combustion plant directive and the air quality standards. Both analyses rely heavily on the work done within the EC Directorate General (DG) XII's ExternE project (European Commission-DG XII, 1995 and 1999). The Environment Directorate (DG XI) of the EC has also started training courses in CBA for their administrative staff to promote better priority setting. Thus, there is an increased interest in using environmental valuation both for CBA, environmental costing and environmental accounting.

International organisations like the OECD, the World Bank and regional development banks and UNEP (United Nations Environment Program) have produced guidelines on environmental valuation techniques; *e.g.*, OECD (1989, 1994 and 1995); Asian Development Bank (1996), and UNEP (1995, Chapter 12). In many cases they have used valuation techniques as an integral part of CBA of investment projects, *e.g.*, the World Bank's evaluation of water and sanitation projects (Whittington, 1998). UN's statistical division UNSTAT has also actively supported the development of resource accounting systems (*e.g.*, the Handbook on Integrated Environmental Economic Accounts). Even though there have been numerous environmental valuation studies of biodiversity and ecosystem functions in the US and in Europe (see Navrud, 1992 and 1999 for an overview of European valuation studies), the policy use of valuation studies seems to have concentrated on air and water pollution impacts and policies (Navrud and Pruckner, 1997). Increased policy use of environmental valuation estimates increases the need for more original studies of environmental goods and health effects from air, water and soil pollution, and improved techniques for transferring valuation estimates from one geographical area and context to another area and context (*i.e.*, benefit transfer techniques).

4. Benefit transfer approaches and their reliability

There are two main approaches to benefit transfer:

1. **Unit Value Transfer**:

   • Simple unit transfer;

   • Unit Transfer with income adjustments.

2. **Function Transfer**:

   • Benefit Function Transfer;

   • Meta analysis.

4.1. Unit value transfer

Simple unit transfer is the easiest approach to transferring benefit estimates from one site to another. This approach assumes that the well being experienced by an average individual at the study site is the same as that which will be experienced by the average individual at the policy site. Thus, we can directly transfer the mean benefit estimate (*e.g.*, mean WTP/household/year) from the study site to the policy site.

For the past few decades such a procedure has often been used in the United States to estimate the recreational benefits associated with multipurpose reservoir developments and forest management. The selection of these unit values could be based on estimates from only one or a few valuation studies considered to be close to the policy site, or based on mean values from literature reviews of existing values. Walsh *et al.* (1992, Table 1) presents a summary of unit values of days spent in various recreational activities, obtained from 287 CV and TC studies. More recently the US Oil Spill Act recommends transfer of unit values for assessing the damages resulting from small "Type A" spills or accidents using the National Resource Damage Assessment Model for Coastal and Marine Environment. This model transfers benefit estimates from various sources to produce damage assessments based on limited physical information from the spill site.

The obvious problem with this transfer of unit values for recreational activities is that individuals at the policy site may not value recreational activities the same as the average individual at the study sites. There are two principal reasons for this difference. First, people at the policy site might be different from individuals at the study sites in terms of income, education, religion, ethnic group or other socio-economic characteristics that affect their demand for recreation. Second, even if individuals' preferences for recreation at the policy and study sites were the same, the recreational opportunities might not be.

Unit values for non-use values of *e.g.*, ecosystems from CV studies might be even more difficult to transfer than recreational (use) values for at least two reasons. First, the unit of transfer is more difficult to define. While the obvious choice of unit for use values are consumer surplus (CS) per activity day, there is greater variability in reporting non-use values from CV surveys, both in terms of WTP for whom, and for what time period. WTP is reported both per household or per individual, and as a one-time payment, annually for a limited time period, annually for an indefinite time, or even monthly payments. Second, the WTP is reported for one or more specified discrete changes in environmental quality, and not on a marginal basis. Therefore, the magnitude of the change, should be close, in order to get valid transfers of estimates of mean, annual WTP per household. Also the initial levels of environmental quality should be close if one should expect non-linearity in the benefit estimate or underlying physical impacts.

For health impacts the question of which units to transfer seems somewhat simpler. With regard to mortality the unit would be the Value of a Statistical Life (VSL) or the more recent and disputed measure of Years of Life Lost (YOLL). For morbidity, it is more complicated since several units of value are used. For light symptoms like coughing, headaches and itching eyes, symptom days (defined as a specified symptom experienced one day by one individual) are often used. Values for more serious illnesses are reported in terms of value per case. However, the description of these different symptoms and illnesses varies in terms of *e.g.*, severity. A better alternative would therefore be to construct values for episodes of illness defined in terms of symptoms, duration and severity (in terms of restrictions in activity levels, whether one would have to go to the hospital, etc.).

On the issue of units to transfer, one should also keep in mind that often the valuation step is part of a larger damage function approach, where we are trying to find values for the endpoints of dose-response and exposure-response functions for environmental and health impacts, respectively, due to changes in *e.g.*, emission of air pollutants. Thus, a linkage has to be developed between the units the endpoints are expressed in, and the unit of the economic estimates. This has been done successfully for *e.g.*, changes in visibility range (Smith and Osborne, 1996), but is more difficult as complexity of changes in environmental resources increase.

The simple unit transfer approach is not fit for transfer between countries with different income levels and standard of living. Therefore, unit transfers with income adjustments have been applied, by *e.g.*, using Purchasing Power Parity (PPP) indexes. However, this adjustment will not take care of differences in preferences, environmental conditions, and cultural and institutional conditions between countries. Very few studies have tested for the impacts on valuation of these other factors. Ready *et al.* (1999) conducted the same CV study in five European countries (the Netherlands, Norway, Portugal Spain and United Kingdom). They found that the transfer error in valuing respiratory symptoms was ±38 per cent in terms of predicting mean willingness-to-pay (WTP) to avoid the symptom in one country from the data of the other countries. The WTP estimates were adjusted with PPP indexes (for the cities the studies were conducted in, since national PPP indexes were not representative for these specific cities). Thus, the remaining differences are due to other factors than income/ purchasing power.

This study is also a test of the accuracy of benefit transfer. The observed transfer error should be compared with the variability in the original estimate within a country of ±16 per cent (estimated using Monte Carlo simulations). These results relate to valuation of respiratory symptoms that can be linked to air or water pollution, and might not be transferable to environmental goods. Thus, we should perform similar types of validity tests of international benefit transfer for both use and non-use value of environmental goods.

4.2. Function transfer

Benefit Function Transfer

Instead of transferring the benefit estimates, the analyst could transfer the entire benefit function. This approach is conceptually more appealing than just transferring unit values because more information is effectively transferred. The benefit relationship to be transferred from the study site(s) to the policy site could again be estimated using either revealed preference (RP) approaches like TC and HP methods or stated preferences (SP) approaches like the CV method and Choice Experiments (CE). For a CV study, the benefit function is

$$WTP_i = b_0 + b_1 G_{ij} + b_2 C_i + e \qquad (1)$$

where $WTP_i =$ the willingness-to-pay of household i, $G_{ij} =$ the characteristics of the environmental good and site j, and $C_i =$ characteristics of household i, and b_0, b_1 and b_2 are parameters and e is the random error.

To implement this approach the analyst would have to find a study in the existing literature with estimates of the parameters b_0, b_1, b_2, b_3 and b_4. Then the analyst would have to collect data on the four independent variables at the policy site. The values of these independent variables from the policy site and the estimates of b_0, b_1, b_2, b_3 and b_4 from the study site would be replaced in the CV model (1), and this equation could then be used to calculate households' willingness-to-pay at the policy site.

The main problem with the benefit function approach is due to the exclusion of relevant variables in the bid or demand functions estimated in a single study. When the estimation is based on observations from a single study of one or a small number of recreational sites or a particular change in environmental quality, a lack of variation in some of the independent variables usually prohibits inclusion of these variables. For domestic benefit transfers, researchers tackle this problem by choosing the study site to be as similar as possible to the policy site. The exclusion of methodological variables makes the benefit function approach susceptible to methodological flaws in the original study. In practise researchers tackle this problem by choosing scientifically sound original studies.

Meta-analysis

Instead of transferring the benefit function from one valuation study, results from several valuation studies could be combined in a meta-analysis to estimate one common benefit function. Meta-analysis has been used to synthesise research findings and improve the quality of literature reviews of valuation studies to come up with adjusted unit values. In a meta-analysis original studies are analysed as a group, where the results from each study are treated as a single observation into new analysis of the combined data set. This allows us to evaluate the influence of the resources' characteristics, the features of the samples used in each analysis (including characteristics of the population affected by the change in environmental quality), and the modelling assumptions. The resulting regression equations explaining variations in unit values can then be used together with data collected on the independent variables in the model that describes the policy site to construct an adjusted unit value. The regression from a meta-analysis would look like equation (1), but with one added independent variable C_s = characteristics of the study s (and the dependent variable would be WTP_s = mean willingness-to-pay from study s).

Smith and Kaoru's (1990) and Walsh et al. (1990 and 1992) meta-analyses of TC recreation demand models, using both summary of TC and CV studies for the US Forest Service's resource planning program, were the first attempts to apply meta-analysis to environmental valuation. Later there have been applications to HP models valuing air quality (Smith and Huang, 1993), CV studies of both use and non-use values of water quality improvements (Magnussen, 1993), CV studies of groundwater protection (Boyle et al., 1994), TC studies of freshwater fishing (Sturtevant et al., 1995), CV studies of visibility changes at national parks (Smith and Osborne, 1996), CV studies of morbidity using Quality of Life Years (QUALY) indexes (Johnson et al., 1996), CV studies of endangered species (Loomis and White, 1996), CV studies of environmental functions of wetlands (Brouwer et al., 1997), and HP studies of aircraft noise (Schipper et al., 1998). Only the last two studies are international meta-analyses, including both European and North American studies. All the others, except Magnussen (1993), analyse US studies only.

Many of these meta-analyses of relatively homogenous environmental goods and health effects are not particularly useful for benefit transfer even within the US, where most of these analyses has taken place, because they focus mostly on methodological differences.* Methodological variables like "payment vehicle", "elicitation format", and "response rates" (as a general indicator of quality of mail surveys) in CV studies, and model assumptions, specifications and estimators in TC and HP studies, are not particularly useful in predicting values for specified change in environmental quality at the policy site. This focus on methodological variables is partly due to the fact that some of these analyses were not constructed for benefit transfer (e.g., Smith and Kauro, 1990; Smith and Huang, 1993; and Smith and Osborne, 1996) and partly because there was insufficient and/or inadequate information reported in the published studies with regard to characteristics of the study site, the change

---

* Carson et al. (1996) is an example of a meta analysis of different environmental goods and health effects, which was performed with the sole purpose of comparing results from valuation studies using both stated preference (CV) and revealed preference methods (TC, HP, defensive expenditures and actual market data).

in environmental quality valued, and income and other socio-economic character-istics of the sampled population. Particularly, the last class of variables would be necessary in international benefit transfer, assuming cross-country heterogeneity in preferences for environmental goods and health effects.

In most of the meta-analyses secondary information was collected on at least some of these initially omitted site and population characteristics variables or for some proxy for them. These variables makes it possible to value impacts outside the domain of a single valuation study, which is a main advantage of meta-analysis over the benefit function transfer approach. However, often the use of secondary data and/or proxy variables introduces added uncertainty, *e.g.*, using income data for a regional population in lack of income data for fishermen at the study site. On the other hand, this secondary data are more readily available at the policy site without having to do a new survey.

Most meta-analyses caution against using them for adjusting unit values due to potential biases from omitted variables and specification/measurement of included variables. To increase the applicability of meta-analysis for benefit trans-fer, one could select studies that are as similar as possible with regards to method-ology, and thus be able to single out the effects of site and population characteristics on the value estimates. However, it is a problem that there are usu-ally so few valuation studies of a specific environmental good or health impact, that one cannot to do a statistically sound analysis.

4.3. *Accuracy of benefit transfer*

While there are very detailed guidelines, although disputed, on how to carry out high-quality original valuation studies, *i.e.*, Arrow *et al.* (1993) for Contingent Val-uation (CV) surveys, no such (universally accepted) guidelines exists for benefit transfer. Smith (1992) has called for the development of a standard protocol or guidelines for conducting benefit transfer studies. Recent studies comparing ben-efit transfers with new CV studies of the same site to test the validity of benefit transfer provide valuable input in the development of such guidelines.

Loomis (1992) argues that cross-state benefit transfer in the US (even for iden-tically defined activities) are likely to be inaccurate, after rejecting the hypotheses that the demand equations and average benefits per trips are equal for ocean sport salmon fishing in Oregon versus Washington, and for freshwater steelhead fishing in Oregon versus Idaho. Bergland *et al.* (1995) and Downing and Ozuno (1996) used the benefit function transfer and unit value approaches. Downing and Ozuno only looked at use value, while Bergland *et al.* also cover transfer of non-use value.

Bergland *et al.* (1995) conducted the same CV study of increased use and non-use values for water quality improvements at two Norwegian lakes (let us call them A and B for simplicity), constructed benefit functions for A and B, and then transferred the benefit function of lake A to value the water quality improvement in lake B, and vice versa. The mean values were also transferred and compared with the original CV estimate, since the two lakes are rather similar with regard to size and type of pollution problem. When selecting the independent variables for the demand function two different approaches were used: *i*) selecting variables which give the largest explanatory power, and *ii*) selecting variables for which it is possible to obtain data at the policy site without having to do a costly survey. The last approach would ease future transfers, but could give less reliable estimates. Several tests for transferability were conducted, but all indicate lack of transferability statistically speaking (*i.e.*, transferred and original values are significantly different at the 5% level). However, the mean values differ by "only" 20-30 per cent, and for many uses (*e.g.*, cost-benefit analysis) this level of accuracy could be acceptable. In one lake the transferred values were highest, in the other they were lower than the estimate from the original study. Thus, from this study one cannot conclude on what procedure would produce the highest values.

While Bergland *et al.* (1995) test benefit transfers spatially by conducting two CV studies at the same time, Downing and Ozuno (1996) test benefit transfer both spatially and intertemporally through CV and TC models of recreational angling at eight bays along the Texas coast. Using a 5 per cent significance level, they found that 91-100 per cent of the estimates were not transferable across bays (but 50-63% of within-bay estimates were transferable across time). Like Bergland *et al.* (1995) they conclude that geographical benefit transfer is generally not statistically reliable. Brouwer and Spaninks (1999) reached the same conclusion in their CV studies of use and non-use values of amenities (meadow birds and flowery ditch-sides) of two Dutch peat meadow sites. The original CV study gave significantly higher estimates than transferred CV estimate from the other peat meadow area, but only 20 per cent difference in mean WTP/household/year in the benefit function transfer. In their international benefit transfer test Ready *et al.* (1999) found that the transfer error in valuing respiratory symptoms (that could be caused by air and water pollution) of ±38 per cent. Whether errors of this size are acceptable depend on the policy use of the value estimates. This could be acceptable in a CBA, but the cost of doing a new valuation study has to be compared with the potential loss of making the wrong decision when using the transferred estimate.

5. Potential for increased policy use of original and transferred value estimates

Results from validity tests show that the uncertainty in benefit transfers both spatially and temporally could be quite large. Thus, benefit transfer should be applied to uses of environmental valuation where the demand for accuracy is not too high. This means using benefit transfer in cost-benefit analyses of projects and policies, but be more careful in using transferred values in environmental costing

31

and accounting exercises, and in particular Natural Resource Damage Assessments (NRDA) and calculations of compensation payments in general.

Benefit transfer is less than ideal, but so are most valuation efforts in the sense that better estimates could be obtained if more time and money were available. Analysts must constantly judge how to provide policy advice in a timely manner, subject to the resource constraints they face. Benefit transfer methods may be particularly useful in policy contexts where rough or crude economic benefits may be sufficient to make a judgement regarding the advisability of a policy or project. Therefore analysts should compare the benefits of increased accuracy of the benefit estimates (when going from a benefit transfer exercise to a new, original valuation study) with the costs of making the wrong decision based on the benefit transfer estimate.

There are five main difficulties or challenges in benefit transfer:

1. Availability and quality of existing studies.

2. Valuation of new policies or projects in respect of:

   • expected change resulting from a policy is outside the range of previous experience;

   • most previous studies valued a discrete change in environmental quality; how can that be converted into marginal values to value the new policy;

   • most previous studies value an increase in environmental quality; how can that be converted to value decrements in environmental quality.

3. Differences in the study site(s) and policy site that are not accounted for in the specification of the valuation model or in the procedure used to adjust the unit value.

4. Determination of the "extent of the market". To calculate aggregated benefits the mean benefit estimate has to be multiplied by the total number of affected households (i.e., households that find their well-being affected by the change in the quality of the environmental good). There is a need for guidelines on how to determine the size of the affected population.

5. While original valuation studies can be constructed to value many benefit (or cost) components simultaneously, benefit transfer studies would often involve transfer and aggregation of individual components. Simply adding them assumes independence in value between the components. If components are substitutes or complements, this simple adding-up procedure would over- and under-estimate the total benefits (or costs), respectively. Thus, correction factors to take these interdependencies into account have to be applied, see Santos (2000) for empirical estimates of such correction factors for rural amenities. Whether it is possible to construct general sets of correction factors that can be applied in benefit transfer is yet to be seen.

The policy response to these main challenges in benefit transfer could be: i) development of improved benefit transfer techniques and a protocol for benefit transfer (including guidelines on how to determine the "size of the market"), and (ii) database of environmental valuation studies. Recently there have been great advances on both these issues. Based on a review of value transfer studies and validity tests of transfer, Brouwer (2000) propose a seven-step protocol for good practice when benefit transfer is used in CBAs. The web-based database EVRI (Environmental Valuation Reference Inventory, *www.evri.ec.gc.ca*/EVRI/) now contains about 700 valuation studies. The majority of these studies are from North America, but the number of European and Asian studies captured in this database is steadily increasing (see also Navrud, 1999 for a favourable evaluation of the suitability of EVRI for capturing European valuation studies). Thus, there is a need to increase the number of existing valuation studies captured in this database, but there is also a need for new, original valuation studies, which have been designed with benefit transfer in mind.

6. Conclusion

This paper has reviewed environmental valuation techniques, that can be used to value rural amenities. Recreational (use) value of rural amenities can be estimated using several valuation methods; both revealed (observed, actual) preferences and stated (expressed) preferences techniques. Unit values, *i.e.*, use value per activity day, for different recreational activities can be transferred from one geographical location to another with transfer errors, which in most cases would be acceptable in cost-benefit analyses. Non-use values of rural amenities expressed as willingness-to-pay to preserve *e.g.*, aesthetic beauty and biodiversity of agricultural landscape have to be based on stated preference techniques, and is in general more difficult and uncertain both to value, transfer and aggregate. The main obstacles to increased policy use of rural amenity values include methodological issues of stated preference methods, lack of valuation studies constructed with benefit transfer in mind, high cost of doing new, original valuation studies, and lack of guidelines for applying benefit transfer approaches and for determining the size of the affected population (which is needed to calculate aggregate benefits).

References

ADAMOWICZ, W.L., BOXALL, P., WILLIAMS, M. and LOUVIERE, J. (1998),
"Stated Preference Approaches for Measuring Passive Use Values: Choice Experiments and Contingent Valuation", *American Journal of Agricultural Economics*, No. 80 (February 1998), pp. 64-75.

ADAMS, R.M. and CROCKER, T.D. (1991),
"Material damages", Chapter IX in Braden, J.R. and Kolstad, C.D. (eds.) (1991): *Measuring the Demand for Environmental Quality*, Elsevier Science Publishers B.V, (North-Holland).

ARROW, K.J., SOLOW, R., LEAMER, E., PORTNEY, P., RADNER, R. and SCHUMAN, H. (1993),
"Report of the NOAA Panel on Contingent Valuation", *Federal Register*, No. 58, pp. 4601-4614, January 15, 1993.

ASIAN DEVELOPMENT BANK (1996),
Economic Evaluation of Environmental Impacts. A Workbook, Parts I and II, Environment Division, Manilla, Philippines, March.

BERGLAND, O., MAGNUSSEN, K. and NAVRUD, S. (1995),
"Benefit Transfer: Testing for Accuracy and Reliability", discussion Paper D-03/95, Department of Economics, Agricultural University of Norway, paper presented at the sixth annual conference of The European Association of Environmental and Resource Economists (EAERE), Umeaa, Sweden, June 17-20, 1995, in Florax, R.J.G.M., Nijkamp, P. and Willis, K. (eds.) (2000): *Comparative Environmental Economic Assessment: Meta Analysis and Benefit Transfer*, Kluwer Academic Publishers.

BOYLE, K.J., POE, G.L. and BERGSTROM, J.C. (1994),
"What do we know about groundwater values? Preliminary implications from a meta analysis of contingent valuation studies", in *American Journal of Agricultural Economics*, No. 76, pp. 1055-1061, December.

BROUWER, R. and SPANINKS, F.A. (1999),
"The validity of environmental benefit transfer: further empirical testing", in *Environmental and Resource Economics*, No. 14(1), pp. 95-117.

BROUWER, R., LANGFORD, I.H., BATEMAN, I.J., CROWARDS, T.C. and TURNER, R.K. (1997),
"A Meta-analysis of Wetland Contingent Valuation Studies", CSERGE Working Paper GEC 97-20, Centre for Social and Economic Research on the Global Environment (CSERGE), University of East Anglia and University College London, 76 pages.

CARLSEN, A.J., STRAND, J. and WENSTØP, F. (1993),
"Implicit Environmental Costs in Hydroelectric Development. An Analysis of the Norwegian Plan for Water Resources", in *Journal of Environmental Economics and Management*, No. 25(3), pp. 201-211.

CARSON, R.C. (1997),
"Contingent Valuation and Tests of Insensitivity to Scope", in Kopp, R., Pommerhene, W. and Schwartz, N. (eds.) (1997): *Determining the Value of Non-marketed Goods: Economic, Psychological and Policy Relevant Aspects of Contingent Valuation Methods*, Kluwer Academic Publishers, Dordrecht, The Netherlands.

CARSON, R.C. (2000),
"Contingent Valuation: A User's Guide", in *Environmental Science and Technology*, No. 34, pp. 1413-1418.

CARSON, R.C., FLORES, N.E., MARTIN, K.M. and WRIGHT, J.L. (1996),
"Contingent Valuation and Revealed Preference Methodologies: Comparing the Estimates for Quasi-Public Goods", in *Land Economics*, No. 72, pp. 80-99.

CARSON, R.C., MITCHELL, R.T., CONAWAY, M.B. and NAVRUD, S. (1997),
Non-Moroccan Values for Rehabilitating the Fes Medina, a report to the World Bank on the Fes Cultural Heritage Rehabilitation Project, August 21, 1997, Department of Economics, UC-San Diego, 238 pages.

DESVOUSGES, W.H, JOHNSON, F.R. and BANZHAF, H.S. (1998),
Environmental Policy Analysis with Limited Information. Principles and Applications of the Transfer Method, New Horizons in Environmental Economics, Edward Elgar, Cheltenham, UK and Northampton, MA, USA.

DOWNING, M. and OZUNO, T. (1996),
"Testing the reliability of the benefit function transfer approach", in *Journal of Environmental and Resource Economics and Management*, No. 30(3), pp. 316-322.

DUBGAARD, A., BATEMAN, I. and MERLO, M. (eds.) (1994),
Identification and Valuation of Public Benefits from Farming and Countryside Stewardship, European Commission, Brussels.

EUROPEAN COMMUNITY (1993),
Towards sustainability: A European Community programme of policy and action in relation to the environment and sustainable development, Office for Official Publications of the European Communities, Brussels.

EUROPEAN COMMISSION–DG XII (1995),
"Externe – Externalities of Energy, Vol. 2: Methodology", European Commission, Directorate General XII Science Research and Development, Report [EUR 16521], EN, Brussels.

EUROPEAN COMMISSION -DG XII (1999),
"Externe – Externalities of Energy, Vol. 7: Methodology, 1998 Update", European Commission, Directorate General XII, Report [EUR 19083], Brussels.

GARP II (1999),
"Final report of the Green Accounting Research Project II to the European Commission – DG XII", RTD Programme "Environment and Climate", Contract ENV4-CT96-0285, November.

JOHNSON, F.R., FRIES, E.E. and BANZHAF, H.S. (1996),
Valuing Morbidity: An Integration of the Willingness-to-Pay and Health Status Index Literatures, December, Triangle Economic Research and Duke University.

LOOMIS, J.B. (1992),
"The evolution of a more rigorous approach to benefit transfer: Benefit function transfer", *Water Resources Research*, No. 28(3), pp. 701-706.

35

LOOMIS, J.B. and WHITE, D.S. (1996),
"Economic benefits of rare and endangered species: summary and meta-analysis", in *Ecological Economics*, No. 18, pp. 197-206.

MAGNUSSEN, K. (1993),
"Mini meta analysis of Norwegian water quality improvements valuation studies", Norwegian Institute for Water Research, Oslo, Unpublished paper, 29 pages.

NAVRUD, S. (1992),
Pricing the European Environment, Scandinavian University Press/Oxford University Press, Oslo, Oxford, New York.

NAVRUD, S. (1994),
"Environmental Costs of Hydro Power Development in Sauda. Results from a Contingent Valuation Study" (in Norwegian), Report to the Norwegian Ministry of Environment.

NAVRUD, S. (1999),
"Pilot Project to assess Environmental Valuation Reference Inventory (EVRI) and to Expands Its Coverage to the EU" Report to the European Commission, DG XI-Environment, July 1, 1999.

NAVRUD, S. and PRUCKNER, G.J. (1997),
"Environmental Valuation – To Use or Not to Use? A Comparative Study of the United States and Europe", in *Environmental and Resource Economics*, No. 10, pp. 1-26.

NAVRUD, S. and VEISTEN, K. (1997),
"Using contingent valuation and actual donations to bound the true willingness-to-pay", presented at the Seventh Annual Conference of the European Association of Environmental and Resource Economists, Lisbon, June 27-29, 1996, Revised version, May 1997.

NOU (1997),
"27 Cost-Benefit Analysis - Principles for evaluation of public projects and policies" (in Norwegian), Norwegian Ministry of Finance, Oslo.

NOU (1998),
"16 Cost-Benefit Analysis – Guidelines for economic evaluation of public projects and policies (in Norwegian), Norwegian Ministry of Finance, Oslo.

OECD (1989),
Environmental Policy Benefits: Monetary Valuation, Organisation for Economic Co-operation and Development (OECD), Paris, ISBN 92-64-13182-5.

OECD (1994),
Project and Policy Appraisal: Integrating Economics and Environment, Organisation for Economic Co-operation and Development (OECD), Paris, ISBN 92-64-14107-3.

OECD (1995),
The Economic Appraisal of Environmental Projects and Policies. A Practical Guide, Organisation for Economic Co-operation and Development (OECD), Paris, ISBN 92-64-14583-4.

POLLACK, R. and WALES, T. (1987),
"Pooling International Consumption Data", in *Review of Economics and Statistics* No. 69, pp. 90-99.

PRUCKNER, G. (1995),
"Agricultural Landscape Cultivation in Austria: An Application of the CVM", in *European Review of Agricultural Economics*, No. 22, pp. 173-190.

READY, R., NAVRUD, S., DAY, B., DOUBOURG, R., MACHADO, F., MOURATO, S., SPANNINKS, F. and RODRIQUEZ, M.X.V. (1999),
"Benefit Transfer in Europe: Are Values Consistent Across Countries?", Paper presented at the EVE Workshop on Benefit Transfer, Lillehammer, Norway, October 14-16, 1999, EU Concerted Action "Environmental Valuation in Europe" (EVE).

ROWE, R.D., LANG, C.M., CHESTNUT, L.G., LATIMER, D.A., RAE, D.A., BERNOW, SM and WHITE, D.E. (1995),
The New York Electricity Externality Study, Volume I and II, Hagler Bailley Consulting, Inc., Oceana Publications Inc.

SANTOS, J.M.L. (1998),
The Economic Valuation of Landscape Change. Theory and Policies for Land Use Conservation, Edward Elgar, Cheltenham, UK.

SANTOS, J.M.L. (2000),
"Problems and potential in valuing multiple outputs: Measuring the externality and public good aspects of nonfood outputs from agriculture", paper presented at the OECD-USDA workshop "The Value of Rural Amenities: Dealing with Public Goods, Non-market Goods and Externalities", Washington DC, June 5-6, 2000.

SELVANATHAN, S. and SELVANATHAN, E. (1993),
"A Cross Country Analysis of Consumption Patterns", in Applied Economics, No. 25, pp. 1245-1259.

SCHIPPER, Y., NIJKAMP, P. and RIETVELD, P. (1998),
"Why do aircraft noise value estimates differ? A meta-analysis", in Journal of Air Transport Management, No. 4, pp. 117-124.

SMITH, V.K. (1992),
"On separating defensible benefit transfers from smoke and mirrors", in Water Resources Research, No. 28 (3), pp. 685-694.

SMITH, V.K. and HUANG, J.V. (1993),
"Hedonic models and air pollution. Twenty-five years and counting", in Environmental and Resource Economics, No. 3, pp. 381-394.

SMITH, V.K. and KAROU, Y. (1990),
"Signals or noise? Explaining the variation in recreation benefit estimates", in American Journal of Agricultural Economics, No. 72(2), pp. 419-433.

SMITH, V.K. and OSBORNE, L. (1996),
"Do Contingent Valuation Estimates Pass a "scope" Test? A Meta Analysis", in Journal of Environmental Economics and Management, No. 31(3), pp. 287-301.

STIGLER, G. and BECKER, G. (1977),
"De Gustibus Non Est Disputandum", in American Economic Review, No. 67(2), pp. 76-90.

STURTEVANT, L.A., JOHNSON, F.R. and DESVOUSGES, W.H. (1995),
A meta-analysis of recreational fishing, Triangle Economic Research, Durham, North Carolina, USA.

TAMBORRA, M. (1999),
"Towards a Green Accounting System for the European Union: the Contribution of GARP II", in FEEM newsletter No. 2, November, pp. 16-18, Fondazione Eni Enrico Mattei (FEEM), Milano, Italy.

UNEP (1995),
Chapter 12: "Economic values of Biodiversity", in *Global Biodiversity Assessment*, United Nations Environment Program (UNEP), Cambridge University Press, ISBN 0-521-56481-6.

WALSH, R.G., JOHNSON, D.M. and McKEAN, J.R. (1990),
Nonmarket values from two decades of research on recreation demand, Advances in applied micro-economics, Vol. 5, pp. 167-193, JAI Press Inc.

WALSH, R.G., JOHNSON, D.M. and McKEAN, J.R. (1992),
"Benefit transfer of outdoor recreation demand studies, 1968-1988", in *Water Resources Research*, No. 28(3), pp. 707-714.

WHITTINGTON, D. (1998),
"Administering Contingent Valuation Surveys in Developing Countries", in *World Development*, No. 26(1), pp. 21-30.

WENSTØP, F. and CARLSEN, A.J. (1998),
"Using decision Panels to Evaluate Hydropower Development Projects", in Beinet, E and Nijkamp, P. (eds.) (1998): *Multi Criteria Analysis For Land Use Management*, Kluwer Academic Publishers, Dordrecht, The Netherlands.

ZIGLIO, E. (1996),
"The Delphi Method and its Contribution to Decision-Making", in Adler, M. and Ziglio, E. (eds) (1996): *Gazing into the Oracle: The Delphi Method and its Application to Social Policy and Public Health*, Jessica Kingsley, London.

Comments by Mitsuyasu Yabe, National Research Institute of Agricultural Economics, Japan

Thank you very much, Dr. Navrud, for presenting a comprehensive overview of valuation techniques and benefit transfer methods. It gave us a good starting point for our discussion. I'd like to supplement his presentation with two points.

My first comment is concerning benefit transfer. When we estimate a large benefit on a site, can we say the site has a high level of rural amenity? The answer is not always. In order to explain the reason briefly, I'd like to use Figure 1.

In Figure 1, the horizontal axis is the level of amenity and the vertical axis is the quantity of a composite good, or can be regarded as money. The amenity level and composite good are shown along with the indifference curve of an individual. If the amenity level increases from Q_1 to Q_2, the willingness-to-pay (WTP) to get Q_2 is given by the distance $P_1.P_2$, and if the amenity level increases from Q_1 to Q_4, WTP to get Q_4 is given by $P_1.P_4$. Thus, the more amenity level increases, the greater WTP is, as Q_4 is higher than Q_2 and $P_1.P_4$ is longer than $P_1.P_2$.

Next, we shall examine another case. Now, assume there are two people, and one lives in the lower amenity level Q_1 and the other lives in the higher amenity level Q_2. Even if the increase of amenity from Q_1 to Q_2 is the same increase from Q_3 to Q_4, the first person's WTP to get Q_2, given by $P_1.P_2$, is much larger than the other's

Figure 1. **Diagram of change in the level of amenity**

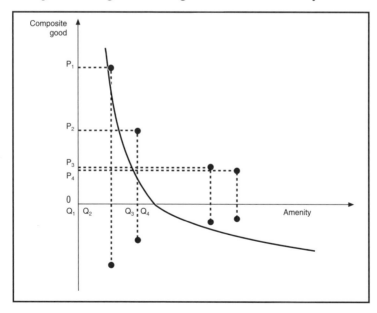

WTP to get Q_4, given by $P_3\text{-}P_4$. Thus, WTP in the lower level of amenity is larger than that in the higher level for the same change of amenity. So when we consider benefit transfer using the results of each CV estimate, we have to read each assumption and situation carefully. For the benefit transfer model we need two variables to show each amenity level and how these amenity levels have changed.

The second comment is the information effect on policy cost to conserve amenity. In the CV survey, it is well known that the information in a survey effects WTP. The policy cost information, however, is important for citizens to decide how much to pay for rural amenity with balancing costs and benefits. I'd like to discuss this point using our case study.

We estimated the value of the headwater conservation forest for Yokohama City. Yokohama City is one of the largest cities in Japan and has almost 4 million citizens. The forest supplies 10 per cent of the total water Yokohama City needs. It costs about ¥2.6 million per year to conserve and manage the forest and ¥200, or about $2, per household. We have compared two groups. In order to conserve this forest, one group was asked for WTP without the information of policy cost and finally 238 samples were analysed. The other group, 185 samples, was asked for WTP with the information. The former had ¥3 642 as the mean WTP and the latter had ¥1 573, and the difference in mean WTP was significant at the level of 0.01 per cent.

The results bring forward some interesting points. Firstly, the information of real policy cost affected WTP. In this case, as the real cost was ¥200 and WTP without information was ¥3 642, we can say that WTP with information was estimated as lower benefit. However, we can say that estimated WTP with information was higher than the WTP without information, if higher cost, for example, ¥6 000 or so, was given.

Secondly, WTP with information is higher than the real maintenance cost. Thus, we can say that Yokohama citizens accepted the present conservation policy. Indeed, from the view point of CV survey, policy cost information might have a bias. For the purpose of political decision making, however, it would be useful to show cost information.

Thirdly, this ¥200 includes only maintenance cost for headwater. However, once we lost this forest, we would have to pay more cost to reforest additionally to get the same benefit. Thus, the estimated benefit should include the greater value than this maintenance cost, namely, the value of multi-functionality of the forest, that is biodiversity, recreation, flood control, and so on. Therefore, when we compare the estimated value and the policy cost, we need to consider what the estimated benefit includes and what the policy cost does not cover.

Chapter 3

Problems and Potential in Valuing Multiple Outputs: Externality and Public-Good Non-Commodity Outputs from Agriculture

by
José Manuel Lima e Santos
Department of Agricultural Economics and Rural Sociology,
Technical University of Lisbon

1. Policy context

There are multiple ways through which rural land contributes to social welfare. The supply of food and raw materials, groundwater recharge, open space for recreation, wildlife habitats, scenic experience, cultural identity, rural employment, rural-community viability and national food security are only some examples of such multiple functions of rural land.

Using a significant share of rural land, agriculture has had a major influence on these multiple functions, although there might be alternative suppliers for some. There typically is a certain degree of jointness in the production of multiple outputs from rural land. For example, changing the agricultural production process to increase the performance of rural land in commodity production (*e.g.*, food, raw materials) usually modifies the levels of other (non-commodity) outputs of rural land, such as landscape, wildlife habitat or water quality. These changes in agriculture are typically caused, in the first place, by market or policy changes. On the other hand, actively promoting particular non-commodity outputs, *e.g.*, by means of environmental policy, can change the competitiveness of commodity production, as well as the levels of other non-commodity outputs from the same land.

The fact that many non-commodity outputs of rural land have externality and public-good characteristics may lead to market failure, *i.e.*, price-signals from markets for the inputs and commodity outputs of land do not generally ensure that a welfare-maximising bundle of commodity and non-commodity outputs is selected.[1]

Because of joint production of commodity and non-commodity outputs, and the possibility of market failure, multifunctionality of agriculture is a relevant issue for all policies that have an effect on the multiple-output bundle from rural land. Examples of such policies are agricultural, environmental, rural-development, food-security, urban-development, energy and transport policies.

There is, in principle, a role for public policy in moving that output bundle so as to improve social welfare. However, it is necessary to make sure that policy failure does not amplify market failure, by moving the bundle of multiple-outputs of rural land in the wrong direction, or too far in the right direction. There are two types of strategy to avoid this policy failure:

1. to avoid direct policy intervention, by creating market or quasi-market mechanisms (*e.g.*, entrance fees) which capture the value of non-commodity outputs of land (or part of it) so as to produce the right incentives for voluntary supply decisions; this, eventually, leads to internalise this value into the workings of the whole economy, through a series of (automatic) multiple-market effects;

2. to explicitly value the multiple, commodity and non-commodity, outputs of land, so that it is possible to design policies for welfare-increasing moves of that multiple-output bundle, or even to select a welfare-maximising bundle.

The complexities of valuation and full cost-benefit analysis implied by option (2) and the practical difficulties in implementing optimal solutions and finding adequate policy tools have led economists and policy makers to check the potential of strategy (1). OECD (2000*b*) work on the multifunctionality of agriculture explores this potential in different situations as regards the particular public-good characteristics of the non-commodity outputs of land. Market or quasi-market mechanisms also promise to harness the potential of rural amenities to improve rural-development prospects in many areas, namely those that are economically marginal from a strictly agricultural point of view (OECD, 1999*a*).

At least for pure public goods, (2) remains the only possible option for policy, in which case only valuation can prevent us from getting into one of the two variants of policy failure referred to above (*i.e.*, moving in the wrong direction, or moving too far beyond the optimum bundle).[2]

According to the discussion above, valuation should be particularly helpful in informing some types of policy decision. An example of these decisions concerns policies aimed at enhancing the performance of rural land with respect to commodity outputs while, at the same time, leading to unintended (positive or negative) changes in non-commodity outputs (environment, rural employment, etc.), especially when these latter outputs have pure-public-good characteristics. This is the case of decisions on agricultural policy reform and trade liberalisation, as these potentially lead to both positive and negative non-commodity effects – *e.g.*, reduced pollution levels from declining fertiliser use; or higher fire risk and loss of valued cultural landscape attributes following farmland abandonment. This is also the case of decisions on whether to go ahead with public or private projects improving the commodity potential of rural land, with both positive and negative effects on non-commodity goals – *e.g.*, water projects for dry regions, which may produce regional employment and stable water provision jointly with degradation of wildlife habitat.

Another major public-policy area requiring valuation to avoid policy failure is that of agri-environmental schemes, which aim at meeting increased public demand for environmental quality, biodiversity and cultural attributes of rural land. Although policy issues in this area are currently dominated by the need for more precise targeting and more effective delivery of real environmental benefits, the ultimate criterion is whether these benefits actually offset policy costs (Willis and Garrod, 1994). This is an evaluation task clearly requiring valuation. Also in the context of agri-environmental policy, valuation could help designing particular schemes so as to get an optimal mix of commodity and non-commodity outputs from the targeted rural land.

The sustainability of economic development, namely rural development, is a third policy issue that may require the valuation of non-commodity outputs of rural land. The greening of national, regional and firm accounts may become a powerful tool to drive economic development along a sustainable path. Green accounts require taking account of changes in natural capital assets over time and aggregating across assets to estimate natural capital depreciation. These are tasks clearly requiring valuation.

Economic valuation can also be put to some uses in the context of market and quasi-market solutions for the externalities of rural land. As it provides demand information, valuation can be used for pricing non-commodity outputs of land (*e.g.*, entrance-fee levels for farmland managed for nature conservation), for example to maximise revenue, which can then be invested in conservation or used to meet other non-commodity goals (Pearce, 1999 and Ward and Beal, 2000).[3]

Policy issues referred to above require weighting multiple policy effects with different natures and expressed in different units. Weighting effects makes it is possible to say whether a change with both positive and negative effects is globally desirable, or even to select an optimal multiple-effect bundle. Weighting is only unnecessary if there is a single non-inferior option (one that is the best in every single respect). However, this will be very unlikely in the context of policies affecting multifunctional land, where multiple (positive and negative) effects often result. Thus, multiple trade-offs between effects need often to be assessed, to select the best course of action or design optimal policy. Assessing these trade-offs requires that all of the effects are valued in a common unit, *i.e.*, that a basic system of weights (values) is developed. As it will become clear later, basing these weights on individuals' willingness-to-pay (WTP) for the policy effects makes the analyst able to select policies that are welfare-improving or even optimal from a social-welfare point of view.

Defining a general frame for valuing the multiple effects of policies affecting rural land requires that these effects be specified in a general way. This is a task for the next section. The example of a policy aimed at non-commodity goals is used for this purpose. Eventually, it is shown that all of the relevant policies referred to above produce the same generic types of effect.

2. The valuation problem

Policies aimed at non-commodity goals for rural land have some generic types of effect. Specifying these effects is essential to understand the nature of the valuation problem at stake.

Some of these policies (*e.g.*, agri-environmental schemes) use financial incentives and depend on voluntary uptake by farmers or other land users, who are required to comply with particular management constraints (fertiliser use, stocking rates, etc.) or to supply specified levels of non-commodity outputs (stone-walls, public access, farm-level employment, etc.). The first step of the policy effects is uptake by farmers. A minimum uptake is required for the policy to have any effect on the targeted non-commodity outputs. Uptake depends on financial-incentive levels as compared to costs of complying with the scheme's requirements. It also depends on scheme design and interactions with other policies (*e.g.*, general agricultural policy support), which may increase the private cost for farmers of entering the scheme.

Still for voluntary schemes, the second step of the policy effects determines the degree of farmers' compliance with the scheme's requirements, which, in this case, were agreed upon between the farmer and the public agency managing the scheme. If the regulatory command-and-control approach is used (*e.g.*, nitrate pollution policy in the EU), compliance is actually the first step of the policy effects. Major monitoring and surveillance problems exist in ensuring full compliance given, the disperse nature of agents and production/environmental processes (*e.g.*, non-point source pollution).

The third step consists of the farm-level adjustments in the production process determined by compliance with the scheme. Four types of physical outcomes result, in general, from these adjustments: 1) changes in the targeted non-commodity outputs; 2) changes in other (non-targeted) non-commodity outputs; 3) changes in commodity outputs; and 4) changes in inputs. Changes (1) are precisely those aimed by the particular scheme, whereas (2), (3) and (4) occur because commodity and non-commodity outputs of land are jointly produced from a same input mix.

Three types of end-product effects follow these adjustments in production at the farm level. The first has to do with the farmer's income. If unbound by management constraints or the requirement to supply non-commodity outputs, farmers are supposed to chose the particular combination of commodity outputs and variable input levels that maximises profit (in fact, the quasi-rent accruing to fixed inputs, such as land and family labour). If bound by those constraints, farmers would maximise profit subject to these constraints. A restricted profit function will be maximised instead of the unrestricted one. Thus, farmer's income will generally decline as a result of complying with the scheme. This income decline is the farm-level compliance cost for farmer i:

$$\Delta y_i \left(\mathbf{p}, \mathbf{w}, \mathbf{q}_i^C \mid T_i \right) = \Pi^C(\mathbf{p}, \mathbf{w}, \mathbf{q}_i^C \mid T_i) - \Pi(\mathbf{p}, \mathbf{w} \mid T_i) \qquad (1)$$

Where $\Pi^C(.)$ and $\Pi(.)$ are the restricted and unrestricted profit functions[4] respectively; $\mathbf{p}$ is the vector of prices of the N commodity outputs; $\mathbf{w}$ is the vector of prices of variable inputs; and $\mathbf{q}_i^C$ is the vector of constraints that farmer i voluntarily agreed to comply with or that were imposed on him by regulation. T_i is for technology, stressing that both profit functions (hence compliance cost) depend on technology. This allows for cost-saving possibilities based on policy-led technological developments. Keeping technology constant, compliance costs depend on prices and the levels of constraints, hence on levels of non-commodity outputs produced as a result of policy.

In voluntary schemes, a farmer will only agree with constraints $\mathbf{q}_i^C$ if induced by a policy payment offsetting Δy_i (assuming farmers are indifferent to non-priced non-commodity outputs). So, in this case, the net income change for farmers is non-negative or even strictly positive (implying policy rents for farmers, i.e., overcompensation). On the other hand, tax-payers' income is reduced to raise funds so that it is possible to compensate farmers for compliance costs and to pay for the administrative costs of the policy (administrative costs need to be paid for also in the case of regulatory schemes). If management constraints are imposed by regulation, farmers actually suffer the whole negative income change in (1).

The second type of effect following adjustments at the farm level comprehends the environmental cause-effect linkages stemming from every single farmer's compliance with constraints $\mathbf{q}_i^C$ and leading to the production of the environmental non-commodity outputs desired by society (and targeted by the scheme), plus environmental unintended side-effects (e.g., a scheme to conserve a traditional arable landscape might increases soil erosion). These are complex ecological processes, most of them known with a high level of uncertainty. Targeted and side-effect environmental outputs are included in the vector $\mathbf{z}$ of non-commodity outputs, with each z_m depending on management

45

constraints q_i^C imposed on all farmers (i=1...F) plus a vector of site-specific environmental factors e_m:

$$z_m = \varphi_m(q_1^C,..., q_F^C, e_m) \tag{2}$$

Each of the environmental production functions, $\varphi_m(.)$, may work at a spatial scale different from that of the farm. It can work at the landscape scale for aesthetic, recreation or wildlife-habitat effects, the catchment scale for water-quality effects, or the global scale for genetic diversity conservation or climatic change. The fact of each environmental non-commodity output of land being produced at a different spatial scale and the uncertainty about environmental production functions create difficult problems for policy evaluation, but not necessarily for valuation. At this stage, it is sufficient to note that the environmental non-commodity outputs directly affecting social welfare are the end-products z, and *not* their farm-level inputs q_i^C's. So, it would be more appropriate to start the valuation step at the z's (not at the q_i^C's) and to take into account the right spatial scale when valuing each z_m.

The third type of cause-effect linkages following farm-level adjustments in production comprehends the general-equilibrium effects of changes in commodity-output supply and input demand. Some of the end-products of these multiple-market effects might be the objectives of the policy scheme itself (*e.g.*, rising local employment, or improving food security). In these cases, these effects are included in the vector z of non-commodity outputs of multifunctional land to be valued. Other end-products of these general-equilibrium effects are unintended side-effects, which may have a positive or negative effect on people's well-being. These end-products typically are price changes, although there might also emerge unintended side-effect changes in employment elsewhere in the economy (possibly in a different country, through trade effects). Prices of commodity outputs change if policy-induced aggregate changes in supply are sufficiently large. OECD (2000c) gives a simple graphical illustration of a rise in the price of a commodity output produced in fixed proportions with a negative externality when this externality is subject to taxation. Provided that aggregate changes in input demands are also sufficiently large, input prices change as well (*e.g.*, fertiliser price declines if many farmers are offered attractive management agreements to reduce fertiliser use).

Changes in commodity output and input prices have feedback effects on farmers' incomes, so complicating the expression used in (1) to compute the compliance cost for farmers.

Although being an unintended side-effect of a policy with non-commodity goals, output-price changes affect consumers' well-being. Hence, valuing these price changes is, of course, a task for the valuation step.

Summarising all the steps of the policy effects reviewed so far, we have: 1) uptake of the scheme by farmers; 2) compliance with agreed management constraints; 3) farm-level adjustments when commodity and non-commodity outputs are jointly produced from a same input-mix; 4) farmers' and others' income changes; 5) general-environmental-interaction effects; and 6) general-equilibrium effects. After having followed all these steps, we are left with three types of end-products, which directly affect the level of well-being of individuals in society:

- changes in non-commodity output levels (either intended or not, environmental or other) from z^0 to z;

- changes in income levels of every single individual i (*e.g.*, farmers, taxpayers, etc.) from y_i^0 to y_i;

- changes in prices of commodity outputs of agriculture (and other prices that change through general-equilibrium effects) from p^0 to p.

This means we can include all the ways through which a policy for multifunctional land affects social welfare by describing the *policy outcome* as a change from (p^0, y_i^0, z^0) to (p, y_i, z). These two states are subsequently referred to as the policy-off and policy-on states.[5]

The next step of policy evaluation is the valuation step. This is aimed at putting a value (or weight, as seen above) in the several end-product effects of a policy, so that the trade-offs between positive and negative effects can be assessed and the best course of action selected.

The policy setting explored so far in this section is focused on policies with non-commodity goals. Other policy decisions, such as agricultural policy reform and trade liberalisation may also require the use of valuation. These decisions refer to a different policy setting. However, the relevant types of generic end-product effects of policy are exactly the same. Differences between these settings have to do with the particular end-product effects that are associated with the main policy goal versus those taken as unintended side-effects. For example, for agricultural policy reform and trade liberalisation the focus is on commodity price changes, which will deliver the expected efficiency gains throughout the whole multiple-market economic system; unintended side-effects are now the related (positive and negative) changes in the non-commodity outputs of multifunctional land (amenity, rural employment, etc.). This inversion (with respect to the policy setting previously explored) of what is considered policy goal and side-effect is totally irrelevant here, as the criterion for a policy effect to be considered in the valuation step is whether it affects social welfare, *not* whether it is among the explicit goals of policy.

3. The basic valuation model

As shown above, multifunctional land generates multiple commodity and non-commodity outputs, which affect the individuals' well-being in different ways

47 |

and through different cause-effect linkages.[6] Having an effect on social welfare is the common theme to all commodity and non-commodity outputs that need to be valued. Thus, both types of output can be analysed within a same valuation frame. By considering, within the same frame, all the ways through which a policy for multifunctional land affects social welfare, we can arrive at a meaningful overall statement about the net welfare effect of such policy.

This is the quintessence of complete cost-benefit analysis of policies with multiple effects on social welfare, including non-market effects such as environmental changes or changes in risk levels faced by individuals (*e.g.*, transportation or food-safety policies). In this sense, there is nothing new or specific about valuing the multifunctionality of land. Indeed, most results in this paper apply to multiple-effect policies in general, even if effects are produced by different economic activities, and hence they do not necessarily imply the multifunctionality of agriculture or any other single activity. Yet, an issue that may be specific to the valuation of the multiple outputs of land is its strong spatial dimension.

The proposed common valuation frame for the multiple outputs of land is based on the assumption that each individual's level of well-being (utility) depends on the levels of consumption of two types of goods: commodity outputs $\mathbf{x}_i = (x_{i1}, x_{i2}, ..., x_{iN})$ bought in the market at prices $\mathbf{p} = (p_1, p_2, ..., p_N)$, and non-commodity outputs $\mathbf{z} = (z_1, z_2, ..., z_M)$ available at zero-price and given quantity/quality:[7]

$$U_i (x_{i1}, x_{i2}, ..., x_{iN}, z_1, z_2, ..., z_M) = U_i (\mathbf{x}_i, \mathbf{z}) \tag{3}$$

Each individual is also assumed to allocate income y_i to the different N commodity outputs so as to maximise own utility given prices $\mathbf{p}$ and exogenous non-commodity outputs $\mathbf{z}$. Differently from levels of commodity outputs $\mathbf{x}_i$, which are selected by the individual at given market prices, non-commodity output levels $\mathbf{z}$ enter the individual's choice problem as determined by the decisions of others (farmers, government, etc.), *i.e.*, as *externalities*. Introducing the selected utility-maximising bundle of commodity outputs $\mathbf{x}_i^*(\mathbf{p}, y_i, \mathbf{z})$ back into the utility function yields the maximum, or *indirect utility function*:

$$V_i (\mathbf{x}_i^*(\mathbf{p}, y_i, \mathbf{z}), \mathbf{z}) = V_i (\mathbf{p}, y_i, \mathbf{z}) \tag{4}$$

Suppose there is a policy affecting the multiple commodity and non-commodity outputs of land, with *policy outcome* described as a change from $(\mathbf{p}^0, y_i^0, \mathbf{z}^0)$ to $(\mathbf{p}, y_i, \mathbf{z})$. Different individuals may be differently affected by policy. For example, income changes may be positive for some and negative for others (reflected in the Δy_i for the particular individual i). Likewise, some individuals may not suffer some of the policy effects, which happens *e.g.*, when the changed z_m's are local public goods, such as the quality of a landscape for its residents (this is way we need to consider different utility functions for different individuals; in this case, local dwellers and others). However, the utility change for individual i is, in general, a result of all three types of policy effects:

$$\Delta V_i = V_i^1 - V_i^0 = V_i\,(\mathbf{p}, y_i, \mathbf{z}) - V_i\,(\mathbf{p}^0, y_i^0, \mathbf{z}^0) \tag{5}$$

If the decision on whether to go ahead with the policy is to be made based on the aggregate-welfare criterion, we should go ahead if:

$$\sum_{i=1}^{I} \Delta V_i > 0 \tag{6}$$

As each individual's utility change in (5) cannot be measured so as to sum up over individuals, this criterion is usually not applicable in practice. However, we can still use an indirect money measure for each individual's utility change. The *compensating variation* (CV$_i$) *of income* is one such a measure. It is defined as:

$$V_i\,(\mathbf{p}, y_i - CV_i, \mathbf{z}) = V_i\,(\mathbf{p}^0, y_i^0, \mathbf{z}^0) \tag{7}$$

i.e., it is the precise amount that needs to be taken from the individual's income, at the policy-on state, to make him or her as well off as at the policy-off state.

If i is a gainer with the policy (*i.e.*, if $\Delta V_i > 0$), then CV$_i > 0$ and represents the maximum the individual would pay for the policy to go ahead (maximum willingness-to-pay, WTP). If i is a loser (*i.e.*, if $\Delta V_i < 0$), then CV$_i < 0$ represents the minimum the individual would require as compensation for the policy to go ahead (minimum willingness-to-accept, WTA). If all individuals gain (or loose) with the policy, we can still use the criterion in (6) even if we cannot measure each individual's utility change. However, in general, some individuals will gain ($i \in G$) and others will lose ($i \in L$). If this is the case, we can algebraically sum the compensating variation across all individuals, *i.e.*:

$$\sum_{i=1}^{I} CV_i = \sum_{i \in G} CV_i - \left| \sum_{i \in L} CV_i \right| = B - C \tag{8}$$

With the first term on the RHS ($B = \sum_{i \in G} CV_i$) representing aggregate maximum WTP of the gainers, or the project aggregate benefits, and the second term ($C = |\sum_{i \in L} cv_i|$) representing aggregate minimum WTA of losers, or the project aggregate costs. If the algebraic sum of compensating variation is positive (*i.e.*, aggregate benefits exceed aggregate costs), we can conclude that, with the policy, gainers are able to fully compensate losers and still remain better off than without it. This is known as the *Kaldor compensation test*. It is a check on whether the particular policy leads to a potential Pareto improvement: if the policy passes this test and the mentioned post-policy distribution of income occurred, some people would be made better off with no one being made worse off. This is the basic criterion we generally use to aggregate benefits and costs across individuals in cost-benefit analysis of public policy.

When a policy affecting multidimensional land causes multiple changes in prices, income and non-commodity-output levels, the compensating variation of individual i can be explicitly defined as:

$$CV_i (\mathbf{p}, y_i, \mathbf{z}, \mathbf{p}^0, y_i^0, \mathbf{z}^0) = y_i - y_i^0 + e_i(\mathbf{p}^0, V_i^0, \mathbf{z}^0) - e_i(\mathbf{p}, V_i^0, \mathbf{z})$$
$$= y_i - e_i(\mathbf{p}, V_i^0, \mathbf{z}) = y_i - e_i(p, V_i(\mathbf{p}^0, y_i^0, \mathbf{z}^0), \mathbf{z}) \qquad (9)$$

Where $e_i(\mathbf{p}, V_i, \mathbf{z})$ is the *restricted expenditure function*, which gives the minimum amount the individual needs to spend on commodity outputs, in order to achieve the utility level V_i, when prices are at $\mathbf{p}$ and non-commodity-output levels at $\mathbf{z}$. [For utility-maximising individuals: $y_i^0 = e_i(\mathbf{p}^0, V_i^0, \mathbf{z}^0)$].

Differentiating CV_i with respect to the prices of commodity outputs yields the vector including the negatives of the Hicksian (compensated) demands for all commodity outputs:

$$\partial CV_i(.)/\partial \mathbf{p} = -\partial e_i(.)/\partial \mathbf{p} = -\mathbf{x}^C(p, V_i^0, \mathbf{z}) \qquad (10)$$

Differentiating it with respect to the levels of non-commodity outputs, we get the vector including the Hicksian (compensated) marginal-value (inverse demand) functions for all non-commodity outputs:

$$\partial CV_i(.)/\partial \mathbf{z} = -\partial e_i(.)/\partial \mathbf{z} = \pi^C(\mathbf{p}, V_i^0, \mathbf{z}) \qquad (11)$$

4. Demand interactions and aggregation across policy effects

Perhaps the most important single valuation issue that is specific to multiple-effect policies is that of demand interactions between policy effects. As it will be shown in this section, these interactions may cause severe aggregation problems when summing up values over different policy effects. This aggregation problem does *not* depend on the way the multiple effects were generated (*e.g.*, on jointness in production) but simply on demand-side considerations.

To start with, note that demands for commodity outputs in (10) depend not only on own and other commodities' prices but also on levels of non-commodity outputs. This allows for interactions in demand between commodities, and between each commodity and each non-commodity output. We say two commodities a and b are substitutes (complements) when the demand for a is increased (reduced) by an increase in b's price, *i.e.*, if:

$$\partial x_a^C (.) /\partial p_b = -\partial^2 CV_i(.)/\partial p_a \partial p_b > (<) \, 0 \qquad (12)$$

Likewise, we say that a commodity a and a non-commodity output b are substitutes (complements) if demand for a is reduced (increased) by an increase in the level of non-commodity output b, *i.e.*, if:

$$\partial x_a^C (.) /\partial z_b = -\partial^2 CV_i(.)/\partial p_a \partial z_b < (>) \, 0 \qquad (13)$$

The corresponding demand interactions based on inverse demands for non-commodity outputs in (11) are as follows. We say two non-commodity outputs a and b are substitutes (complements) when the marginal value of a is reduced (increased) by an increase in the level of b, i.e., if:

$$\partial \pi_a^c (.) / \partial z_b = \partial^2 CV_i(.)/\partial z_a \partial z_b < (>) \, 0 \qquad (14)$$

We say that a non-commodity output b and commodity a are substitutes (complements) if the marginal value of b is increased (reduced) by an increase in a's price, i.e., if:

$$\partial \pi_b^c (.) / \partial p_a = \partial^2 CV_i(.)/\partial z_b \partial p_a > (<) \, 0 \qquad (15)[8]$$

Totally differentiating equation (9) yields:

$$dCV_i = dy_i - \sum_{n=1}^{N} \partial e_i(.)/\partial p_n . dp_n - \sum_{m=1}^{M} \partial e_i(.)/\partial z_m . dz_m \qquad (16)$$

Integrating for the overall (multiple-price, multiple-non-commodity-output) change yields:

$$CV_i (.) = \int_0^{CVi} d\theta = \int_{yi0}^{yi} d\theta \; - \qquad (17)$$

$$-\sum_{n=1}^{N} \int_{pn0}^{pn} \partial e_i(p_1, \ldots, p_{n-1}, \bullet, p_{n+1}{}^0, \ldots, p_N{}^0, V_i{}^0, z^0)/\partial\bullet \, . \, d\bullet \; -$$

$$-\sum_{m=1}^{M} \int_{zm0}^{zm} \partial e_i(p, V_i{}^0, z_1, \ldots, z_{m-1}, \bullet, z_{m+1}{}^0, \ldots, z_M{}^0)/\partial\bullet \, . \, d\bullet$$

Or:

$$CV_i (.) = \int_0^{CVi} d\theta = \int_{yi0}^{yi} d\theta \; + \qquad (18)$$

$$+\sum_{n=1}^{N} \int_{pn}^{pn0} \partial e_i(p_1, \ldots, p_{n-1}, \bullet, p_{n+1}{}^0, \ldots, p_N{}^0, V_i{}^0, z^0)/\partial\bullet \, . \, d\bullet \; +$$

$$+\sum_{m=1}^{M} \int_{zm0}^{zm} - \partial e_i(p, V_i{}^0, z_1, \ldots, z_{m-1}, \bullet, z_{m+1}{}^0, \ldots, z_M{}^0)/\partial\bullet \, . \, d\bullet$$

Taking into account (10) and (11) we notice what is happening in equation (18):

- demands for commodity outputs are integrated over own price, from policy-on (final) to policy-off (initial) price levels, which will produce a negative (positive) result for price rises (decreases), *i.e.*: a cost (benefit) for the consumer;

- marginal value functions of non-commodity outputs are integrated over the output level from policy-off (initial) to policy-on (final) output levels, which will produce:

    - a positive (negative) result (*i.e.*, a benefit or cost, respectively) for a non-commodity output rise (decrease), when this output is a positive externality;

    - a negative (positive) result (*i.e.*, a cost or benefit, respectively) for a non-commodity output rise (decrease), when this output is a negative externality.

Note also that we are integrating demands and marginal-value functions along a well defined sequence: we started by the income change, then we integrate demands for commodities from 1 to N, and, eventually, inverse demands for non-commodity outputs are integrated from 1 to M. At each integration step we used the following rule:

set price/output levels for price/output changes that were *previously integrated at their policy-on* (*i.e.*, *final*) *levels*; for price/output changes that are to be *subsequently integrated*, set them *at their policy-off* (*i.e.*, *initial*) *levels*.

This rule generates what is known as a sequential valuation of the multiple-price, multiple-output change. In Annex 1 we verify that these sequential values are additive by solving the integrals in (18) and comparing with the definition of compensating variation in (9).

If we define the income change as Δy_i, the sequential values of price changes as SV_{in}, and the sequential values of changes in non-commodity output levels as SV_{im}, *i.e.*:

$$(\Delta y_i) = \int_{yi0}^{yi} d\theta = y_i - y_i^0 \qquad (19)$$

$$SV_{in} = \int_{pn}^{pn0} \partial e_i(p_1, ..., p_{n-1}, \theta, p_{n+1}^0, ..., p_N^0, V_i^0, z^0)/\partial\theta \cdot d\theta$$

$$SV_{im} = \int_{zm0}^{zm} -\partial e_i(\mathbf{p}, V_i^0, z_1, ..., z_{m-1}, \theta, z_{m+1}^0, ..., z_M^0)/\partial\theta \cdot d\theta$$

We can write equation (18) in the simplified form:

$$CV_i = \Delta y_i + \sum_{n=1}^{N} SV_{in} + \sum_{m=1}^{M} SV_{im} \tag{20}$$

This is a very important result and it is independent of the particular sequence we use. We may integrate over prices and non-commodity outputs in whatever sequence we wish, provided we follow the rule for sequential paths stated above. This property of compensated money measures such as CV_i is known as path-independency. The proof is presented *e.g.*, by Johansson (1987).

Aggregating equation (20) across individuals, as in (8), to investigate whether the policy is a potential Pareto improvement (Kaldor compensation test), *i.e.*, whether it passes the benefit-cost test, we get:

$$\sum_{i=1}^{I} CV_i = \sum_{i=1}^{I} (\Delta_{yi} + \sum_{n=1}^{N} SV_{in} + \sum_{m=1}^{M} SV_{im}) =$$

$$\sum_{i=1}^{I} \Delta_{yi} + \sum_{n=1}^{N} \sum_{i=1}^{I} SV_{in} + \sum_{m=1}^{M} \sum_{i=1}^{I} SV_{im} = \tag{21}$$

$$\Delta y + \sum_{n=1}^{N} SV_n + \sum_{m=1}^{M} SV_m$$

with Δy being the aggregate net change in personal incomes in the whole economy, SV_n being the integral of the aggregate demand for commodity n, and SV_m the integral of the aggregate inverse demand (marginal value) for non-commodity output m. This means that, when using the correct rule for sequential valuation, we can either 1) integrate individual demands, sum up over commodity and non-commodity outputs, and then aggregate across individuals (as in the first line of 21), or, simply, 2) integrate aggregate demands and sum up over commodity and non-commodity outputs (as in the third line of 21).[9]

This useful result shows that demand interactions are *not* a concern for summing up values over individuals, but only when summing up values over policy effects. This is intuitive, as demand interactions between policy effects are *internal* to each individual. Thus, the issues of aggregating across individuals and across policy effects are largely separable.

Note, however, that this useful result only holds when using the correct rule (above) for sequential valuation. Yet, very often, we have *not* sequential values for each price/non-commodity-output change but independent values (IV_{in}, IV_{im}), which are values secured as if the particular price/non-commodity-output change was the next modification to the status quo (policy-off) state (p^0, y_i^0, z^0), i.e.:

$$IV_{in} = \int_{pn}^{pn0} \partial_{ei}(p_1^0, \ldots, p_{n-1}^0, \theta, p_{n+1}^0, \ldots, p_N^0, V_i^0, z^0)/\partial\theta.d\theta \tag{22}$$

$$IV_{im} = \int_{zm0}^{zm} -\partial_{ei}(p^0, V_i^0, z_1^0, \ldots, z_{m-1}^0, \theta, z_{m+1}^0, \ldots, z_M^0)/\partial\theta.d\theta \tag{23}$$

Summing up over effects yields the independent valuation and summation (IVS) result for individual i:

$$IVS_i = \int_{yi0}^{yi} d\theta \;_{+\ldots} \tag{24}$$

$$+ \sum_{n=1}^{N} \int_{pn}^{pn0} \partial_{ei}(p_1^0, \ldots, p_{n-1}^0, \theta, p_{n+1}^0, \ldots, p_N^0, V_i^0, z^0)/\partial\theta \cdot d\theta$$

$$+ \sum_{m=1}^{M} \int_{zm0}^{zm} -\partial_{ei}(p^0, V_i^0, z_1^0, \ldots, z_{m-1}^0, \theta, z_{m+1}^0, \ldots, z_M^0)/\partial\theta \cdot d\theta$$

which is in general different from the true money measure defined in equation (9), i.e.:

$$IVS_i \neq CV_i \tag{25}$$

because the useful result on the additivity of values, which is stated in equations (18) to (20) and demonstrated in Annex 1, only applies to sequential values, i.e., when the integrals are evaluated according to the sequential rule above. This result does not hold for independent values. Hence, summing up independent values across policy effects (price and non-commodity-output changes), either before or after aggregating across individuals, is prone to an aggregation bias known as the IVS bias, whose magnitude is given by:

$$IVS_i - CV_i \tag{26}$$

Or, in per cent form:

$$100 \times (IVS_i / CV_i) - 100$$

The sign of the IVS bias depends on the sign and magnitudes of the substitution effects defined in equations (12) to (15). It is, in general, unknown because there may be offsetting effects between substitution and complementary effects.

In simpler cases, something can be said on the sign of the IVS bias if we know something about the underlying substitution relationships. One such case is that of a regulatory-based change in only non-commodity outputs (landscape, biodiversity, downstream water quality, and so on), which are valued by the non-farming population and are sufficiently small to have no effect on market prices of commodity outputs. Farmers will suffer the negative income changes defined in (1) and are supposed indifferent to the non-commodity outputs generated by policy. In this case, the only demand interactions to be considered are those between non-commodity outputs for the non-farming population. If all the non-commodity outputs z to be supplied by the policy are substitutes (complements) for each other, the IVS bias will be positive (negative). This is because in the (correct) sequential valuation procedure, marginal value functions for each non-commodity output are shifted down (up) along the sequence, as more and more substitutes (complements) are added. This is not taken into account by independent valuation. Thus, in this case, summing up independent values leads to overvaluing (undervaluing) the multiple-output change. When all non-commodity outputs z are independent in demand from each other, the IVS bias is nil. If some are substitutes and other complements, it may (very unlikely) happen that all effects cancel out each other, in which case the IVS will be nil as well.

The importance of the IVS bias is very often underestimated in practice. It may be one of the greater (if not the greatest) limitations to valuation and cost-benefit analysis of multiple-effect policy changes, because:

- most usual valuation methods, either when original valuation studies are used or when the analyst uses valuation information transferred from previous studies, are prone to this bias;

- this bias may be sufficiently large to lead to the wrong policy recommendations in many practical cases (we refer to tests of the policy implications of bias as importance tests, as opposed to usual tests of the statistical significance of bias).

It can be theoretically (*i.e.*, generally) shown that, when large numbers of non-commodity outputs are considered, IVS will overstate the unbiased value of the entire multiple-output policy. The proof is given by Hoehn and Randall (1989), who used a single-household general-equilibrium model to investigate whether substitution and complementarity actually cancel out in such large-numbers situations, and demonstrated that this was not the case. As the number of outputs becomes large, IVS will lead to overvaluation of the entire multiple-output policy, *i.e.*, the substitution effect prevails in large-numbers cases. Hoehn and Randall's proof is somehow intuitive, and based on the fact that the unbiased overall compensating variation of the multiple-output policy (defined in equation 9) is bounded above by the productive capacity of the economy, whereas IVS is not. They also stress the potential for 'too many proposals passing the benefit cost test' when each of many individual agencies *independently* evaluates its own projects as if they were the next change to the status quo.

However, substitution may not characterise all pair-wise demand interactions between non-commodity outputs. Hoehn and Randall's result does not apply to predicting the sign and magnitude of each particular pair-wise demand interaction, which, in cases of smaller numbers of outputs, is required to predict the sign of the IVS bias.

Even in this context of smaller numbers of policy effects, Hoehn (1991) suggested that substitutes should be more frequent than complements. Santos (1998) derived the Slutsky equations for multiple-output policies to show that two non-commodity outputs that are complements in preferences[10] can be substitutes in demand (as defined in equation 14) provided the income effect is sufficiently large. Large income effects seem to be generally implied by the empirical evidence on multiple-output changes reviewed by Santos (1998). This reinforces the idea that IVS will very often lead to overvaluation in cases of small numbers of non-commodity outputs as well as (though probably less severely than) in large-numbers cases. Hoehn (1991) and Hoehn and Loomis (1993) explicitly tested this hypothesis, which was supported by the empirical evidence.

Some results from four CVM studies in Portugal and the UK (Almeida, 1999; Madureira, 2000; and Santos, 1998), which were designed to take into account demand interactions, also enable us to test this hypothesis by directly comparing the IVS result with that of the unbiased aggregation procedure in (18) for a number of multiple-non-commodity-output bundles in different contexts. These results also enable us to check whether there is a trend for the IVS bias to grow with the number of non-commodity outputs in the bundle that we are valuing. The survey and modelling approach used to produce these results are technically described in Santos (1998).[11] The relevant results from the 4 CVM surveys are presented in Table 2.

Some preliminary words to introduce the four CVM studies are required. The Pennine Dales Environmentally Sensitive Area (ESA) study (Santos, 1998), carried out in 1995, comprised 422 usable questionnaires administered to visitors to the area, with each visitor being asked weather he or she would pay some specified amounts for some particular mixes of three basic programmes (Programme 1 was stone wall and field barn conservation; Programme 2 was the conservation of flower diversity and ground nesting birds in hay meadows; and Programme 3 was the conservation of small broad-leaved woods). All of these programmes were defined so that programme implementation would conserve the corresponding landscape and biodiversity resources at current levels as opposed to some degree of degradation forecasted for the near future. Programmes need to be separable in production so that each programme bundle is an available alternative for management or policy. This required for the results to be useful in identifying the optimal policy bundle.

The Peneda-Gerês National Park (NP) study (Santos, 1998) was carried out in 1996 and comprised 704 usable questionnaires administered to NP visitors. Survey design was almost exactly the same as in the previous study but the three programmes were slightly different, to fit the relevant conservation issues in this Portuguese NP: Programme 1 was now about the conservation of terraced farming in the lower slopes of the NP; Programme 2, about the conservation of traditional irrigated meadows, and Programme 3, about the conservation of farm-owned oak woodland in the NP.

The Sintra-Cascais Natural Park (NP) study (Almeida, 1999) was carried out in 1999. It was aimed as a survey pilot with only 76 usable questionnaires administered to NP visitors. Survey design comprised different mixes of 5 basic conservation programmes, involving the conservation of windmills, traditional vineyards planted in sand dunes, scarce remains of broad-leaved woods, a globally endangered plant species, and two nationally endangered species of birds of prey, respectively. Models to secure the marginal value of each programme yielded surprisingly high levels of statistical significance given the small number of observations. Yet, as regards demand interactions only that between woodland and birds of prey could be efficiently estimated. Thus, we only present estimated demand interactions with respect to these two policy outputs.

The Douro Superior study (Madureira, 2000) was carried out in 1998 and 1999 and comprised two separate surveys: one of visitors to the area, yielding 796 usable questionnaires, and another of the general public living in towns of Northeast Portugal, yielding 291 usable questionnaires. Both surveys were separately estimated to account for the differences in preferences between visitors and the general public, which included many non-users. Another difference with respect to the three studies above was that survey design comprised only two programmes – 1) the conservation of traditional almond tree orchards in steep slopes, as opposed to land abandonment; and (2) the afforestation of the area currently with almond trees, also as opposed to the abandonment of orchards – which were combined in different area proportions, *e.g.*, 50%:50%, 50%:25% or 25%:0%, where 100% is the area currently with almond trees. Thus it was possible to model WTP for any combination of these land uses plus abandoned area in the remaining % of land (Madureira, 2000). This enables us to compare, in Table 2, the demand interactions for the two different populations and for two different such land-use combinations.

The first conclusion to draw from Table 2 is that for all of the 13 multiple-output bundles in Table 2, the IVS bias is positive, implying substitution relationships between the several non-commodity outputs in the bundle. Moreover, all of the estimated IVS biases were found to be statistically significant,[12] *i.e.*, they could not be interpreted as the result of the particular random samples that were selected.

It is also interesting to look for patterns in the size of the IVS bias across different situations as regards the size of the bundle (which varies between 2 and 3 policy outputs), the similarity of the outputs that interact in demand, the amount of each output and different populations.

Estimates from the Pennine Dales ESA case suggest that the IVS bias increases with the size of the bundle, with the most complete bundle (3 outputs) exhibiting the highest IVS bias: 78% as compared to 40-51% for 2-output bundles. Yet, this trend is not confirmed by the Peneda-Gerês NP case, where respondents seem to be prepared to pay a large premium to have the three most important landscape attributes of the area conserved altogether, which may create some complementarity in demand when the third output is included in the bundle. In general we can deduce, from Hoehn and Randall's theoretical result, that as the number of outputs in the bundle grows large the IVS bias will eventually rise, but for such small numbers cases prediction of patterns would require much more empirical research.

We would expect that the more similar two outputs are the more close substitutes they are. This is because similar goods tend to satisfy similar (or the same) needs of individuals. Thus, purely aesthetic/cultural landscape attributes, such as stone-walls, barns and terraces would be poor substitutes for meadows and woods, which were largely perceived by respondents as providing wildlife habitat, not purely aesthetic elements. The results in Table 2 support this prediction, with IVS biases (thus strength of substitution) being larger for 1) woods versus meadows than for 2) meadows or woods versus stone-walls, barns or terraces. This is particularly evident in the first two case-studies, although the high IVS bias for woodland-and-species-preservation in the third case (Sintra-Cascais NP) also confirms this trend.

The fourth case-study allows one to check what happens to the size of IVS bias (thus the strength of demand substitution) when the amount of one of the outputs is increased. Thus, for both visitors and the general public, the IVS bias is significantly increased with the rise from 25 per cent to 50 per cent in the share of afforested land.

The Douro Superior study also enables us to compare the size of the IVS bias between two populations. In fact, substitution between almond tree orchards and afforested land is much stronger for visitors than among the general public. For the former, the value of the output-bundle actually declines with the amount of afforested land, despite the fact that afforested (as compared to abandoned) land is itself a good, *not* a bad.

It is also relevant to ask whether the magnitude of the IVS bias is sufficient to lead to wrong policy decisions being recommended by the cost-benefit analysis,

Table 2. **IVS bias for a series of 4 CVM studies of agricultural landscapes in the UK and Portugal**

Case study	Nb. of outputs	Outputs description	Independent valuation			IVS result	Joint valuation	IVS bias (in %)
			Output 1 (O1)	Output 2 (O2)	Output 3 (O3)			
Pennine Dales ESA in the UK (Santos, 1998)	2	Stone walls (O1) and hay meadows (O2)	43.01	42.62		85.63	61.17	40%
	2	Stone walls (O1) and woodland (O3)	43.01		42.90	85.91	60.20	43%
Currency: 1995 £	2	Hay meadows (O2) and Woodland (O3)		42.62	42.90	85.52	56.61	51%
	3	Stone walls (O1), hay meadows (O2) and woodland (O3)	43.01	42.62	42.90	128.53	72.05	78%
Peneda-Gerês NP in Portugal (Santos, 1998)	2	Terraces (O1) and meadows (O2)	6 221	4 205		10 426	7 253	44%
	2	Terraces (O1) and woodland (O3)	6 221		6 634	12 855	9 029	42%
Currency: 1996 PTE	2	Meadows (O2) and woodland (O3)		4 205	6 634	10 839	6 721	61%
	3	Terraces (O1), meadows (O2) and woodland (O3)	6 221	4 205	6 634	17 060	11 559	48%
Sintra-Cascais NP in Portugal (Almeida, 1999) Currency: 1999 PTE	2	Woodland (O1) and birds of prey (O2)	10 156	6 275		16 431	6 832	141%
Douro Superior in Portugal (Madureira, 2000) Currency: 1998/99 PTE	2	Almond tree orchards 50% (O1) and forest 25% (O2), for visitors	12 981	5 466		18 447	14 078	31%
	2	Almond tree orchards 50% (O1) and forest 50% (O2), for visitors	12 981	8 668		21 649	12 911	68%
	2	Almond tree orchards 50% (O1) and forest 25% (O2), for general public	9 860	3 334		13 194	11 631	13%
	2	Almond tree orchards 50% (O1) and forest 50% (O2), for general public	9 860	5 635		15 495	12 368	25%

i.e., to test the practical importance, as opposed to the statistical significance, of bias. This was possible for the two first case-studies in the table, for which we had estimates of policy costs (Santos, 1998). For the Pennine Dales ESA case, the unbiased social benefit-cost ratios were much over 1.00 for all of the four output-bundles (actually in the range 3.4-6.3). Thus the (overestimated) IVS benefit-cost ratios could only lead to the same policy recommendation as unbiased ones, that is: going ahead with any of those output bundles.[13] Note, however, that this result heavily depends on the particular characteristics of this policy case, in particular the fact that true benefits were here much larger than costs.

In the Peneda-Gerês NP case, the unbiased social benefit-cost ratios for the several output-bundles were in the range 0.65-1.43, with one case at exactly 1.00. Thus, policy recommendations are much weaker here than in the previous policy case. Note, however, that even in this case, IVS biases were not sufficiently large to invert the unbiased policy recommendations. For example, the correct benefit-cost ratio for the terraces-and-meadows bundle was 0.65, whereas the IVS-biased one was 0.93, still below 1.00. On the other hand, for the terraces-meadows-and-woods bundle, the unbiased benefit-cost ratio was estimated as just 1.00, whereas the IVS-biased one is estimated as 1.48, leading to a perhaps too overconfident recommendation of going ahead with the policy. In many cases, especially in complex real-world policy cases where the number of non-commodity outputs of policy is much larger than 2 or 3, the importance of IVS biases will be greater (Hoehn and Randall, 1989).

What recommendations can, therefore, be made to improve usual valuation practice, so as to avoid practically important biases? There are basically two such recommendations.

- One is using a valuation approach, such as that used in the four studies just referred to, which, by jointly valuing the several multiple-output changes, automatically takes into account substitution effects; this is a straightforward way to get the unbiased value of the overall multiple-output bundle (or series of bundles that need to be separately considered so as to select the optimal bundle).

- The other is extending research, using this approach, to different policy contexts, to check if the trends identified above are confirmed and whether some general pattern emerges (see also Randall, 1991); if this is the case, this pattern could be modelled to predict the sign and magnitude of the IVS bias for the specific circumstances of the policy to be evaluated. This would generate adjusting factors, which would eventually help to correct empirical benefit measures estimated by using IVS-bias-prone approaches. This systematic generation of adjusting factors will probably come up as the most cost-effective solution, as most (cheaper) empirical approaches to valuation, especially benefit transfers, are based on piecewise (i.e., independent) valuation of effects followed by summing up across effects (i.e., IVS is used).

5. Approaches to empirical valuation of multiple non-commodity outputs

The main focus in this section is on the available empirical valuation strategies for the non-commodity outputs of multifunctional land, as income and price changes have been the subject of many reviews in the past (*e.g.*, Jus *et al.*, 1982). In particular, we are concerned with ways to value multiple-output changes that take account of demand interactions between outputs.

With respect to multiple price changes, the estimation of demand systems for multiple commodity outputs from market data on prices and quantities might enable analysts to take account of the demand interactions between these outputs defined in equation (12). This requires that the parameters for the relevant cross-price effects are included in the model.[14]

Demand interactions between commodity and non-commodity outputs defined in equation (13) are used as a basis for inferring people's values for non-marketed goods by looking at how changes in these non-marketed goods shift the demand functions of related market commodities. This is the strategy used *e.g.*, by the varying-parameter model (Vaughan and Russell, 1982) and other variants of the travel-cost demand model (TCDM), which aim to go beyond valuing WTP for access to a recreational site, into valuing WTP for quality changes at the site (the relevant non-commodity output here is site quality, *e.g.*, water quality, expected fish catch, or bird diversity).

Demand interactions between non-commodity outputs defined in equation (14) are the ones interesting us the most in this section. Thus, we will briefly review the potential of different valuation methods to value multiple non-commodity outputs of land in ways that take account of demand interactions between these outputs. There are many survey, economic-incentive-mechanism and econometric problems associated with these methods. As most of these problems are general and *not* specific to multiple-output valuation, they are only briefly referred to in what follows.[15] We frame the presentation around a proposed typology for non-market valuation methods, to ensure clarity of vocabulary throughout the discussion, and as a way to systematically identifying and locating specific approaches to multiple-output changes within that typology.

A first criterion to classify non-market valuation methods is the type of empirical data used. There are two fundamentally different types of data. Hypothetical data are about people's expressed values or choices as elicited in response to hypothetical scenarios; behavioural data are about people's actual behaviour in actual settings. Problems with hypothetical data are that people have limited capacity to understand the significant amount of valuation-relevant information that needs to be conveyed during an interview, and to process this information so as to arrive at a considered valuation or choice in a short time period. In addition to these cognitive difficulties, people might adopt strategic behaviour, by giving a self-interested answer aimed at influencing the outcome of the policy decision and that does not necessarily truly reveal their own preferences.[16]

On the other hand, behavioural data have long been preferred by many economists (who sometimes seem to ignore these data also come from questions asked to people) on the grounds that actual decision settings push people to make more considered decisions, as they will actually incur the costs of a wrong choice. Thus, behavioural data would be a more truly reflection of people's preferences. Yet, there are also typical problems associated with behavioural data. Behaviour does not speak for itself. It needs to be interpreted to reveal preferences and values. When modelling behaviour for this purpose, the characteristics of the actual setting that influence behaviour and that are a major concern for valuation (e.g., water quality, landscape attributes, travel cost, etc.) need to be described in ways that correspond to how people actually perceive them. This is because people do not react to objective reality but to the way it is subjectively perceived. If characteristics are not described in perception-consistent ways, models will misinterpret behaviour, which will lead to biased value revelation.

Different data formats result from different ways to put questions to reality. Ordinary market data stems from the observation of pairs of prices and quantities in actual markets. Travel cost methods use similar data, but with one significant difference: the implicit price paid by each individual to accede the site (the travel cost) is not directly observable and needs to be constructed by the analyst based on distance travelled, travel time and assumed prices for distance and time. Data used in hedonic-price models are the observed prices at which units of a complex good (typically houses) are traded in the market and the observed price-affecting attributes (house size, characteristics of the neighbourhood, environmental quality, etc.) of each one of such units.

There are also different formats for hypothetical data, e.g., we may:

1. directly ask people exactly what we need to know, e.g., how much would you be prepared to pay as an entrance fee to a particular recreation site? This is the *open-ended Contingent-valuation-method* (CVM) *format* for valuation questions.

Alternatively we may ask things in indirect ways, such as:

2. would you pay p as an entrance fee to a particular recreation site or prefer not to enter at that price? (with amounts p varying across respondents); this is the *discrete-choice* CVM *format* (Bishop and Heberlein, 1979);

3. if you could choose between having the (policy-on) multiple-output bundle z^1 at price $\$1^1$ or bundle z^0 (policy-off levels) at zero price, what would you choose? (with different respondents being presented different policy-on bundles z^2, z^3,... and different prices $\$p^2$, $\$p^3$,...); this is a *multi-attribute discrete-choice* CVM *format* (Hoehn and Loomis, 1993; and Santos, 1998);

4. if you could choose between having $(\mathbf{z}^1, \$p^1)$, $(\mathbf{z}^2, \$p^2)$, $(\mathbf{z}^3, \$p^3)$ or $(\mathbf{z}^0, \$0)$, what would you choose? Or how would you rank these options by preference order? (with different respondents being presented different choice sets, which always include the policy-off option, *i.e.*, $\mathbf{z}^0$ at price $0); these are the *choice-experiment* and *contingent-ranking formats* respectively (Adamowicz *et al.*, 1994; and Lareau and Rae, 1989).

Format (3) is a particular case of format (4), where the choice-set has only two options.

Note that format (4) has a behavioural counterpart: think *e.g.*, of the actual choice by a recreational fisher among different fishing sites *s* within the available choice set (which always comprehends the decision not to go fishing at zero price), with sites presenting different quality attributes $\mathbf{z}^s$ and different travel costs $\$p^s$.

A second criterion to classify non-market valuation methods is the type of analytical method used to reveal value from available data. There are two different types of such methods: direct and indirect methods. Direct methods require that we have directly asked people about exactly what we need to know, as in data format (1) above. The analysis here is no more than calculating mean (median or other indicator of central tendency of) WTP in the sample of respondents and making some type of statistical inference about the population's mean. Then we aggregate, by multiplying this mean by the total number of people in the population.

All the other data formats referred to above require that a more complex analytical approach be used so as to indirectly reveal values from data.

For example, the travel cost method models the relationship between trip frequency and implicit price of assess to the site (plus other demand-relevant factors), and uses that estimated demand relationship to estimate the value of access to that site for the average visitor (consumer's surplus, or the area under the demand curve). This result is theoretically comparable to WTP for access directly secured by the hypothetical elicitation format (1).[17] As suggested above with respect to the varying-parameter model and similar variants of the TCDM, the travel cost method can also be used to measure WTP for quality changes at the site, which is the most relevant application to measure WTP for landscape, water quality, biodiversity or other non-commodity outputs of land. For this purpose, we need also to measure quality variables $\mathbf{z}$ in a preference-consistent way. Then we need to use these variables as shifters of the estimated demand relationship between trip frequency and travel cost (which requires multiple site data, to get the necessary variation in site quality). Observed change in access value (consumer's surplus difference corresponding to the quality change $\Delta\mathbf{z}$) yields the (use) value of the policy-led quality change $\Delta\mathbf{z}$. Note that WTP for the quality change is here only secured at a second regression step. Thus, with TCDMs, WTP for quality changes is two-steps away from observed data.

63

Another example of an indirect method for value revelation is the hedonic-price method. This is based on a regression modelling approach to uncovering the partial effects of environmental-quality variables or other non-commodity goods z on the prices of complex market goods, such as housing. These (marginal) partial effects are interpreted as the implicit prices of the z's. The inverse demands (marginal values) for the z's are only revealed at a second regression step, where implicit prices for the z's are regressed on individual's characteristics (including income), and the levels of the z's themselves. Thus, as with TCDMs, marginal WTP for quality changes revealed through hedonic-price modelling is also two (regression) steps away from observed data.

The advantage of data formats (1) to (4) is that they enable the analyst to reveal values for quality changes in one single regression step, which is econometrically more efficient, in that it gets more precise estimates of the required marginal WTP for the diverse non-commodity outputs of multifunctional land.

Let us exemplify with data format (1), which corresponds to open-ended CVM data. If we use this data format to directly ask WTP for access to different sites, which offer different bundles z of public-good non-commodity attributes, we can directly model WTP for access as depending on z (site quality) plus income, and other socio-economic determinants of value. This is equivalent to directly estimating the compensating variation function $CV_i(.)$ in equation (9) across individuals i, which requires using individual's socio-economic characteristics c_i as shifters for CV_i to take into account individual-specific preference differences, $i.e.$, we make:

$$CV_i(\mathbf{z}, y_i, \mathbf{z}^0) = y_i - e_i(V_i(y_i, \mathbf{z}^0), \mathbf{z}) = y_i - e(V(y_i, \mathbf{z}^0, \mathbf{c}_i), \mathbf{z}, \mathbf{c}_i) = CV(\mathbf{z}, y_i, \mathbf{z}^0, \mathbf{c}_i) \quad (27)$$

This is an example where the value of access to each site can be *directly* secured (using a simple average), but marginal WTP for quality changes (*i.e.*, for different levels of non-commodity attributes) are *indirectly* secured through a single regression step.

The regression model in (27) can be estimated through ordinary-least-squares (OLS) methodology from continuous WTP data secured with format (1). In the estimated regression model, the parameter estimate for each non-commodity output z_a will give the corresponding marginal value, as defined in equation (11). If included, the parameter for the interaction term $z_a z_b$ will yield the pair-wise substitution effect between a and b (Hoehn, 1991), as defined in equation (14). Note that by using only one regression step we are increasing the efficiency of the estimation of marginal values (inverse demands) for non-commodity outputs, and, especially, that of demand interactions between these outputs.[18]

Note as well that, as in data-format (1) we ask for WTP for access, we are only securing marginal *use* values of non-commodity outputs (as *e.g.*, in Hanley and Ruffell, 1993). Yet, this is *not* an inherent limitation of this approach. If we reframe the valuation question to have something like:

(1a) how much would you be prepared to pay as a tax rise to make sure that environmental quality at National Park X is maintained at z^1 as opposed to degraded to z^0 at no cost?

We may get total economic value for the respondents, including non-use values, and even indirect use values if respondents are made aware of the relevant ecological processes that produce indirect use values, such as wildfire and flood prevention, nutrient cycling and so on.[19]

A more indirect approach needs to be used to model choice data formats (2) to (4), as they produce discrete (censored), as opposed to continuous, information on WTP. For example, a yes (no) answer to question (2) only informs us about whether the particular individual's WTP is above (below) the proposed price amount $p. Two economic theory-consistent approaches are available to estimate WTP from this type of data.[20] We may assume that choices are generated either by i) utility maximisation (Hanemann, 1984), in which case we recover the parameters of the indirect utility function in equation (4); or by ii) expenditure minimisation (Cameron, 1988), in which case we directly recover the parameters of the compensating variation (CV_i) function in equation (9), as with the OLS models for open-ended CVM data just discussed.

Both approaches are equivalent except with respect to the way the random term enters the econometric model (McConnell, 1990).[21] Cameron's approach was used in the case-studies discussed in section 4 (cf. Santos, 1998), as it allows for direct estimation of the demand relationships (substitution effects) between multiple non-commodity outputs in equation (14), provided we include the relevant interactions terms $z_a.z_b$ in the model, as discussed above for the OLS approach. Another example of this type of application is Hoehn and Loomis (1993).

Note that while direct value-revelation methods are generally based on hypothetical data, indirect methods can be applied to either hypothetical or behavioural data. For example, the Random-Utility Model (RUM; cf. McFadden, 1974) used to analyse hypothetical choices generated by question format (4), so as to reveal the marginal values of non-commodity outputs z, is exactly the same as that used to analyse its behavioural-counterpart data (e.g., the fishing-site actual choice example mentioned above). Indeed, Adamovicz et al. (1994) pooled hypothetical and behavioural data with the same format to jointly estimate a single RUM, which has some advantages.

One of these advantages of joint estimation of pooled hypothetical and behavioural data is that the latter rely on actual recreation sites with characteristic-bundles z^s, which naturally induces a strong degree of multi-collinearity among the different characteristics in the bundle across sites. For example water-quality aesthetic attributes may be strongly correlated with trout abundance; hedgerows with pasture as opposed to arable land (e.g., in England); and field trees with other attributes of the "dehesa/montado" agro-ecosystem (in the Iberian Peninsula). Strong multi-collinearity between variables is responsible for a well-known statistical problem: it makes impossible to disentangle the separate marginal effect of each attribute variable on WTP. Thus, the estimated marginal values of each non-commodity good z_m are "artificially" small and statistically insignificant. Introducing interaction terms to estimate and account for demand interactions makes things even worse. An advantage of hypothetical data here is that hypothetical bundles may be designed so as to avoid multi-collinearity between the z's (orthogonal design), thus maximising the efficiency in estimating marginal values and enabling the analyst to introduce interaction terms to account for demand interactions. Joint estimation allows us to take advantage of the strengths of both types of data. For an empirical demonstration of the merits of this strategy, see Adamovicz *et al.* (1994).

All approaches to valuation of the multiple non-commodity outputs of land referred to so far in this section imply that an original valuation study (survey and estimation) is designed so as to match the policy evaluation problem at hand, and implemented to solve this problem. However, what is usual in practical policy evaluation is analysts making resort to previous valuation studies and transferring valuation information from these studies to build the benefit estimate that is required for the policy evaluation problem at hand. This practice is known as *benefits transfer*. This is today's dominant valuation practice because it is cheaper than carrying out an original valuation study for each policy, and, especially, because carrying out such an original study is usually not compatible with the time constraints of the policy process. There are many ways to carry out benefit transfers, some more reliable than others (Desvousges *et al.*, 1998). Summarising, we can either: (1) transfer an unadjusted scalar WTP figure, *i.e.*, a WTP estimate exactly as it is in the original study; (2) adjust this figure, *e.g.*, using a GNP ratio between the original study's and policy-problem's countries, if applicable; or (3) transfer a WTP function, like that in equation (9), estimated at the original study, by re-estimating this function with values for the independent variable that are supposedly representative of the context of the policy to be evaluated. Other transfer techniques involve meta-analysis of multiple relevant WTP estimates in the literature, used to summarise all this wealth of valuation information and predict an estimate for the relevant policy context.[22]

There are many general problems with these transfer techniques (see, *e.g.*, Desvousges *et al.*, 1998; Smith, 1992; McConnell, 1992; and Boyle and Bergstrom, 1992). Yet, one is quite specific of multiple-output policy settings, and hence more relevant for the valuation of policies for multifunctional land. This has to do with the choice between carrying out what Desvousges *et al.* (1998) call disaggregate transfers and aggregate transfers. In disaggregate transfers, we separately look for original studies in the literature for each of the policy effects, separately transfer benefit estimates for each effect, and then sum up across effects. This has the obvious advantage of making the analyst list (hence recalling) all of the policy effects, which leads to completeness in benefit estimation. On the other hand, the procedure is prone to the IVS bias referred to in section 4, which may be large for separate estimation and summation over multiple policy effects.

The alternative is carrying out an aggregate transfer, in which we look for past valuation studies of complex multiple-effect policies similar to the one we need a benefit estimate for, and jointly transfer the original multiple-effect benefit estimate as a whole. The problem is that it is usually impossible to find a past valuation study of a policy that is exactly the same as (or even a good approximation to) the one of interest, with respect to all (or even many) of the policy effects *and* the surveyed population. Another problem is that making people value multiple policy effects in a single step (in the original study) might have (1) led some people to forget about some of these effects (recall errors), or (2) created difficult cognitive problems for people to take into account all policy effects and the corresponding trade-offs in rapid valuation exercises (as in a typical survey). These recall and cognitive errors lead us to the conclusion that while a simultaneous valuation of all of the multiple policy effects, as implied by equation (9), would be theoretically preferable, it may be practically impossible. And this is a limitation not only for benefits transfer but also for original benefit estimation – note that the recall and cognitive errors just referred to relate to the original study, *not* the transfer itself; of course, they are carried over when transferring the original benefit estimate to the policy context at hand. Thus, this is a very general problem in the empirical estimation of benefits of multiple-effect policies, such as policies affecting multifunctional land.

So, it may happen that, in practice, the only possible way forward in many cases is keeping to the practicable IVS procedures, that is: disaggregate transfers as well as original IVS-estimated benefits. But this stresses the need to seriously consider the suggestion, made in section 4, of extending the research on demand interactions to different policy contexts, so that we can search for patterns of IVS biases common to similar contexts. These patterns will lead us to estimate the adjusting factor to be used in each context. These factors could then be systematically applied to correct for the large IVS biases usually incurred in disaggregate transfers, as well as in IVS-based original benefit estimation, when these are the only practical alternatives to estimate the benefits of complex policies affecting the multiple functions of rural land.

6. Conclusions and further issues raised by policy uses

This paper has shown how to develop a coherent frame for the valuation of policies affecting the multiple externality and public-good functions of rural land. Values were defined so as to be fully compatible with values for price and income changes brought about by the same policies. Indeed, the strength of economic-valuation and cost-benefit-analysis language is the coherence and clarity it introduces as regards the meaning of valuation (*i.e.*, what are we valuing?) and the final result of the analysis (*i.e.*, what does optimal policy means? Or: what does policy passing the benefit-cost test means?).

The proposed valuation frame was used to raise and discuss several problems associated with multiple-output valuation, namely demand interactions between multiple non-commodity outputs. Conceptual considerations and empirical evidence led us to identify these demand interactions and an associated aggregation bias (the IVS bias) as some of the greatest challenges in the way to get (unbiased) values for multiple-effect policies.

Moreover, the paper discussed different empirical approaches to non-market valuation, together with the problems and potential of each approach to deal with multiple non-commodity outputs of rural land, and the issue of demand interactions between these outputs. Other, more general, issues with empirical valuation are not specific to multiple-output valuation, and thus were only briefly reviewed in the paper. Further applied research on demand interactions in this context was deemed necessary to raise the policy-evaluation potential of the proposed valuation frame as well as that of the discussed approaches to valuation.

Summing up, and conditional on the future outcome of that research effort on demand interactions, we are lead to consider that available non-market valuation approaches will, in the near future, become completely up to the task of (unbiased) valuation required by several policy uses, which were listed in section 1, namely:

- evaluating policies for agriculture, such as decisions on agricultural policy reform and trade liberalisation, which aim at enhancing the commodity efficiency of the sector, but also lead to (negative or positive) changes in the non-commodity outputs of rural land (environment, local employment, etc.);

- making decisions on whether to go ahead with investment projects, such as *e.g.*, water projects, aimed at improving the commodity potential of rural land, with both positive and negative effects on non-commodity goals;

- evaluating particular agri-environmental schemes, or domestic agri-environmental policy, aimed at meeting social demands for better rural environmental quality;

- contributing to the design of either horizontal agri-environmental schemes or schemes for agriculture and conservation in designated areas (ESAs or EU Natura 2000 sites), so as to get an optimal mix of commodity and non-commodity outputs from targeted land;

- contributing to the measurement of sustainable rural development and the design of policies for sustainable agriculture;

- providing management-relevant demand information (demand schedules; demand dynamics, as related to the evolution of demand determinants) to public or private suppliers of rural amenities, in the context of market and quasi market supply mechanisms.

Meanwhile, as in general there are no better substitutes for non-market valuation in providing the information required by these policy decisions, and subject to some cautions (especially with respect to aggregation biases), the discussion in this paper would recommend to expand the use of these techniques in public-policy evaluation of multidimensionality issues.

In some cases, non-monetary valuation techniques will be a possible approximation. This is, for example, the case with the decision-making problem of a budget-constrained agency aimed at providing the bundle of non-commodity outputs (*e.g.*, recreation facilities) that maximises their clients' welfare. A variant of the data format referred to as (4) in Section 5 (one without price but keeping multiple attributes) was proposed by Kahn *et al.* (1999). This data format can be analysed in the same way as its monetary counterpart referred to in that section.[23] Yet, the fact that we do not get monetary WTP values for the different attributes hinders us to aggregate across individuals or sub-populations, if they have different preferences. In general, non-monetary values have some use limitations as compared to monetary values. For example, using non-monetary valuation in this policy context would require us to assume homogeneous preferences across individuals.

Though using a coherent and clear conceptual frame, and having no perfect substitutes for many policy uses, monetary valuation of the multiple non-commodity outputs of policies affecting rural land has a major weakness: the complexity of detailed considerations that are required for empirical applications (survey, estimation and model-use for value-revelation) to avoid many known possible sources of bias. This can make empirical applications too expensive or, especially, too time-consuming in some cases. In particular this complexity can create serious difficulties for final policy users to fully control the empirical applications they commission to external experts. This stresses the need to establish broadly accepted protocols for each specific use. With respect to valuation of the multifunctionality of land, in a policy context, these protocols should specify proper rules for aggregation over policy effects, based on extensive research on demand interactions between the non-commodity outputs of rural land which is largely still to be done.

Another issue needing further technical refinements for a more efficient application of the proposed non-market valuation frame to the multifunctionality of land is a protocol to identify the relevant non-commodity outputs to be valued in each empirical case. Of course, exclusion of outputs on an *ad hoc* basis makes the approach amenable to all sorts of manipulation. According to the valuation frame proposed in the paper, we should include all outputs with a significant effect on individuals' welfare. Implementing this criterion would require the analyst to undertake some back-of-the-envelope calculations, based on previous benefit estimates in the literature and some previous information about the policy, so as to decide which non-commodity outputs meet the condition to be fully considered in the valuation step. The work of OECD on agri-environmental indicators is giving important steps towards listing the relevant environmental outputs of multifunctional land, in general, and standardising ways to measure them (cf. OECD, 1999*b*, 1999*c*, and OECD forthcoming).

There is a related issue on how non-commodity outputs **z** should be measured for valuation purposes. The discussion in section 5 stresses the need to use perception-consistent definitions and measurements of the z's. Otherwise, we will misinterpret behaviour and get biased value estimates when using behaviour-based methods such as the TCDM. Likewise, if we use hypothetical methods, the description to respondents of the non-commodity outputs in ways that widely diverge from how these people usually perceive such outputs "forces" people to adopt a different view of the decision problem, which may lead to elicit biased values. So, the **z**'s should definitely be defined and measured in perception-consistent (*i.e.*, subjective) ways, at least for valuation purposes. On the other hand, objective measurements of the same **z**'s is required for targeting, monitoring and evaluation purposes, as well as for making management and policy decisions. This creates the need to study how subjective perceptions relate to objective reality, as the only way to establish the required link between valuation results and management recommendations.[24]

Another issue is raised by the frequent reaction of policy makers to the (unexpectedly) large aggregate WTP values usually coming up from valuation studies of non-commodity outputs of rural land (see, *e.g.*, European Commission, 1998). A very frequent concern is that aggregate benefits, namely those secured by the use of CVM followed by multiplication by an estimate of the relevant population seem unbelievably large when compared to policy costs. For example, with respect to a valuation study of the UK's Environmentally Sensitive Areas (ESAs), the European Commission (1998) feels uncomfortable about the fact that "the claim that the UK schemes above secured ECU275 million of benefit for ECU11 million of expenditure seems hard to sustain without qualification". Although this may be a very reasonable feeling, we should add some words to it:

- With public goods, vertical aggregation of marginal values for the same unit of the good (*e.g.*, for an hectare of land, or for an individual of an endangered-species) may lead to unbelievably high (though correct) per unit WTP values for the public-good (*e.g.*, preservation) as compared to WTP for private uses of the same good (*e.g.*, hunting); Bishop and Welsh (1992) illustrate this point with the per-unit preservation value for a small, largely unknown, endangered fish species in the US, which was estimated at an unexpectedly high value per individual fish.

- As we are dealing with goods for which there are no markets, the usual equivalence of marginal benefits and marginal cost of production does not apply (see, *e.g.*, McConnell, 1992); thus, we have no scientific basis on which to base an assessment of whether a scheme's aggregate marginal benefits are disproportionate as compared to marginal cost.

- To get the benefit figure of ECU275 million for the UK's ESA policy as a whole, the European Commission summed up over specific individual ESAs, which, as we have shown in this paper, is prone to the IVS bias – possibly a strong level of bias, as we are here summing over 9 policy components; thus the fact the overall figure resulted "too high" is, at least in some extent, due to an inaccurate aggregation procedure.

- Something needs to be said in favour of the reasonableness of the European Commission's feelings about uncomfortably large benefit estimates. In addition to general problems with valuation methods themselves, there are two serious flaws with many CVM studies of public goods where per-capita WTP figures are simply multiplied by the estimated population to get an aggregate benefit estimate. First, the population estimate may be strongly inaccurate. Second, the sample producing the per capita WTP figure may be non-representative of the population. Both problems are rather serious when we deal with goods with a strong non-use-value component. Smith (1992, 1993) stressed this extent-of-the-market problem. Bateman *et al.* (1999) provide a recent empirical example and show how adequately controlling for 1) the distance-decay in per capita WTP, 2) the spatial distribution of the population around the site, 3) the spatially differentiated socio-economic characteristics of that population, and 4) the increasing non-response rate with distance (it was a mail survey) might reduce the initial aggregate benefit estimate (done as usual) by 75 per cent. Expanding the use of Geographic Information Systems (GIS) to deal with these and many other spatial dimensions of multifunctional land, such as the location of substitute sites (Brainard *et al.*, 1997), appears as the almost perfect solution to deal with many complexities of the empirical valuation of site-specific multiple-outputs, such as those resulting from policies affecting rural land.

- A final issue has to do with a possible limitation of the joint approach to valuing multiple-outputs that was used in the case-studies discussed in section 4. The problem was raised in a recent OECD (2000*b*) paper. This problem is set in a context of multifunctional benefits, illustrated with an example involving both a local public good (use value of landscape for local residents) and a pure public good (non-use values of biodiversity). It is said that, in this case, the suggested approach "*cannot be applied even from a theoretical point of view*", as the "*beneficiaries of the two goods are different, but there could be some consumption relationships between the two goods*".

71

- I would like to show that this problem does not stem from a theoretical impossibility and that it has a straightforward empirical solution based on appropriate survey design. As shown above, demand interactions are internal to each individual. So, for example, the demand interaction between the local and pure-public goods in the example above concerns only local residents. This interaction is, therefore, amenable to the use of the proposed joint approach to multiple-output valuation, through a multi-attribute CVM survey, in this case a survey of the local population. This survey needs then to be complemented by a second, single-issue, survey of the non-residents about the value of the pure-public-good for them. Theoretically (*i.e.*, in general), we can add up the benefits (or even marginal-value curves) secured from separately surveying and modelling each population's benefit, provided that these benefits were modelled in ways that take account of demand interactions (which is the case with the proposed approach). In fact, the issues of aggregating over policy effects (in this case, the local versus pure public goods) and over individuals/populations are independent, as shown by equation (21). Hence, the solution is mainly a matter of correct survey (*i.e.*, questionnaire and sampling) design. A similar solution was actually implemented with respect to the visitor and general public sub-populations in the Douro Superior study (Madureira, 2000), which was referred to in section 4.

Annex I

Demonstration of Additivity of Sequential Values[25]

To demonstrate that sequentially valued price and non-commodity output changes are additive, we solve the integrals in equation (18) to secure:

$$CV_i(.) = y_i - y_i^0 +$$
$$+ e_i(\mathbf{p}^0, V_i^0, \mathbf{z}^0) - e_i(p_1, p_2^0, p_3^0, \ldots, p_N^0, V_i^0, \mathbf{z}^0) +$$
$$+ e_i(p_1, p_2^0, p_3^0, \ldots, p_N^0, V_i^0, \mathbf{z}^0) - e_i(p_1, p_2, p_3^0, \ldots, p_N^0, V_i^0, \mathbf{z}^0) +$$
$$+ e_i(p_1, p_2, p_3^0, \ldots, p_N^0, V_i^0, \mathbf{z}^0) - e_i(p_1, p_2, p_3, \ldots, p_N^0, V_i^0, \mathbf{z}^0) + \ldots$$
$$+ e_i(p_1, p_2, p_3, \ldots, p_N^0, V_i^0, \mathbf{z}^0) - e_i(\mathbf{p}, V_i^0, \mathbf{z}^0) -$$
$$- e_i(\mathbf{p}, V_i^0, z_1, z_2^0, z_3^0, \ldots, z_M^0) + e_i(\mathbf{p}, V_i^0, \mathbf{z}^0) +$$
$$- e_i(\mathbf{p}, V_i^0, z_1, z_2, z_3^0, \ldots, z_M^0) + e_i(\mathbf{p}, V_i^0, z_1, z_2^0, z_3^0, \ldots, z_M^0) +$$
$$- e_i(\mathbf{p}, V_i^0, z_1, z_2, z_3, \ldots, z_M^0) + e_i(\mathbf{p}, V_i^0, z_1, z_2, z_3^0, \ldots, z_M^0) + \ldots$$
$$- e_i(\mathbf{p}, V_i^0, \mathbf{z}) + e_i(\mathbf{p}, V_i^0, z_1, z_2, z_3, \ldots, z_M^0)$$

From the second line onwards, there is a term in each line cancelling out with a term in the following line. Then the all sum above collapses into:

$$CV_i(.) = y_i - y_i^0 + e_i(\mathbf{p}^0, V_i^0, \mathbf{z}^0) - e_i(\mathbf{p}, V_i^0, \mathbf{z})$$

As, for an expenditure-minimising individual, $y_i^0 = e_i(\mathbf{p}^0, V_i^0, \mathbf{z}^0)$, we eventually get:

$$CV_i(.) = y_i - e_i(\mathbf{p}, V_i^0, \mathbf{z})$$

Which demonstrates equality between the sum of sequentially valued changes in prices and non-commodity outputs and the definition of the compensating variation of a multiple-effect policy, in equation (9). This shows the unbiasedness of sequential valuation and summation, as opposed to independent valuation and summation (IVS).

Notes

1. Conditions for market failure in the context of multifunctional agriculture are explored in OECD (2000*b*).

2. This is why we tend to implicitly assume pure-public-good characteristics for non-commodity outputs in the valuation model developed later in this paper.

3. Extending in this direction the model developed in this paper is a complex but not impossible task. Johansson (1987) extends the definition of exact welfare measures to exogenous-priced rationed goods. Congestible goods are particularly difficult to model, as there are two separate problem-dimensions: user congestion (endogenous), which can possibly be solved by quasi-market mechanisms; and the quality of the resource itself, which is probably not amenable to this solution.

4. These restricted and unrestricted profit functions can be derived from underlying production technology for joint commodity and non-commodity (Santos, 1998).

5. The policy-on state is referred to as $(\mathbf{p}, y_i, \mathbf{z})$ and not something as $(\mathbf{p}^1, y_i^1, \mathbf{z}^1)$, which would imply fixed levels, because we want to leave policy-on levels free to change in cases where we want to optimise, *ex ante*, the policy design (as opposed to cases where we need to assess a fixed policy design or to justify, *ex post*, a given policy). Policy-on and off states need not to be static situations. If they are supposed to evolve in time, we have a policy-off time path $(\mathbf{p}^0(t), y_i^0(t), \mathbf{z}^0(t))$ and a policy-on time path $(\mathbf{p}(t), y_i(t), \mathbf{z}(t))$ instead of states. This adds another dimension to the specification of the policy and makes valuation much harder a task.

6. When an output has no (direct or indirect) effect on individuals' welfare it is not considered in this analysis. While excluding truly intrinsic values of nature, this approach still considers a variety of ways though which nature and the environment affect humans, as, for example, the knowledge about the existence of living species and geological features (with extinction or degradation reducing the well-being of some people) or the indirect effects of tropical forests and the seas in regulating climates.

7. This does not imply that there is such a thing as a utility 'figure', but simply that individuals are able to consistently rank all possible bundles $(\mathbf{x}, \mathbf{z})$ according to their preferences.

8. Note that this equation and the corresponding definition are equivalent to those in (13).

9. Note that demands and inverse demands should be aggregated across individuals according to the type of commodity/non-commodity output at issue. Typically, commodities are private goods and demands for these should be horizontally aggregated (*i.e.*, summing amount demanded for each price); on the other hand, non-commodity outputs typically have public-good characteristics; thus, demands should be vertically aggregated (*i.e.*, summing marginal values for each level of the public good) to account for non-rivalry in consumption.

10. That is: complements in consumption, with the increase in one of the non-commodity outputs raising the marginal utility of the other. This relationship in preferences should be very frequent *e.g.*, with landscape attributes that are jointly consumed in one single view.

11. For a summary presentation of the methods and issues, see Santos (1999).

12. Using a simple test by estimating a 95% confidence interval (CI) for the joint valuation result and comparing the estimated upper bound for this CI with the IVS result.

13. Another question is which bundle to select. This is dealt with using a sequential cost-benefit procedure, which is fully explained in Santos (1998) and illustrated in Santos (1999).

14. While the (correct) theoretical frame for valuation developed in sections 3 and 4 is based on compensated demand theory, demand systems estimated from market data are often based on Marshallian (*i.e.*, income-constant, uncompensated) demands. There are two ways to deal with this difference between theoretical concept and empirical practicality. One is invoking Willig's (1976) bounds for this difference, which tell us that, for most practical valuation cases, consumer's surplus (*i.e.*, the area under Marshallian demand curve) will be a sufficient *approximation*. On the other hand, Hausman's (1981) *exact* approach involves integrating Marshallian demands back to the indirect utility function (using Roy's identity), and then deriving compensated welfare measures, as in equation (7).

15. For general reviews of these problems see *e.g.*, Cummings *et al.* (1986), Mitchell and Carson (1989), Carson *et al.*, (1999), Haneman and Kanninen (1998), Bockstael *et al.*, (1991), and Palmquist (1991).

16. On the other hand, strategic behaviour does not always lead to lie about own preferences. It all depends on the incentive-properties of the way the valuation question is framed (Carson *et al.*, 1999).

17. Except that consumer's surplus is an uncompensated money measure and CVM elicits compensated measures.

18. As these require the estimation of the second-order interaction terms just referred to, which rises multi-collinearity problems. More about these problems below in the main text.

19. *i.e.*, assuming they know the ecological production functions in equation (2), or that the end-products z in these equations are, themselves, the object of valuation.

20. As we do not have here continuous information on WTP but only discrete indicators (yes/no or particular discrete choices), *i.e.*: censored information on WTP (*e.g.*, > or <p), we are precluded from using OLS methods to estimate WTP from this type of data. Thus we need to make resort to maximum-likelihood (ML) estimation.

21. .It is added to utility in Hanemann's approach, and directly added to WTP in Cameron's.

22. Santos (1998) tests this meta-analytical approach applied to transfer agricultural landscape values.

23. *i.e.*, using a multi-attribute random-utility model (RUM) estimated by maximum-likelihood (ML).

24. Santos (1998) presents a methodology to establish such a link and an application developed in the practical context of policies for agriculture and the countryside.

25. This annex was adapted from an earlier demonstration by Hoehn (1991), who only considered two non-commodities with no price changes.

References

ADAMOVICZ, W.L., LOUVIERE, J. and WILLIAMS, M. (1994),
"Combining Revealed and Stated Preference Methods for Valuing Environmental Amenities", in *Journal of Environmental Economics and Management*, No. 26, pp. 271-292.

ALMEIDA, Rui (1999),
"Avaliação Contingente de Programas de Conservação: O Caso de Estudo do Parque Natural Sintra-Cascais", Relatório de Fim de Curso de Engenharia Agronómica (submitted to the Technical University of Lisbon).

BATEMAN, Ian J., LANGFORD, Ian H. and NISHIKAWA, Naohito (1999),
"Some Notes on the Aggregation of Benefits Data", presentation at the Workshop on Benefit Transfer/EU Concerted Action on Environmental Valuation in Europe (EVE), Lillehammer, Norway, 14-16 October 1999.

BISHOP, R. and HEBERLEIN, (1979),
"Measuring Values of Extramarket Goods: Are Indirect Measures Biased?", in *American Journal of Agricultural Economics*, 61(5),pp. 926-930.

BISHOP, R. and WELSH, M. (1992),
"Existence Values in Benefit-Cost Analysis and Damage Assessment", in *Land Economics* No. 68(4), pp. 405–17.

BOCKSTAEL, Nancy E., McCONNELL, Kenneth E. and STRAND, Ivar (1991),
"Recreation", in Braden, J. and Kolstad, C. (eds.): *Measuring the Demand for Environmental Quality*, Amsterdam, North Holland, pp. 227-270.

BOYLE, K. and BERGSTROM, J. (1992),
"Benefit Transfer Studies: Myths, Pragmatism, and Idealism", in *Water Resources Research*, No. 28(3), pp. 657-663.

BRAINARD, Julii, LOVETT, Andrew, BATEMAN, Ian, LANGFORD, Ian and POWE, Neil (1997),
"The Use of Geographical Information Systems to Improve Benefit Transfers", unpublished paper, School of Environmental Sciences, University of East Anglia.

CAMERON, T. (1988),
"A New Paradigm for Valuing Non-market Goods Using Referendum Data: Maximum Likelihood Estimation by Censored Logistic Regression" in *Journal of Environmental Economics and Management*, No. 15, pp. 355-379.

CARSON, Richard T., GROVES, Theodore and MACHINA, Mark J. (1999),
"Incentive and Informational Properties of Preference Questions, Plenary Address to the 9th Annual Conference of the European Association of Resource and Environmental Economists, Oslo, Norway, June 1999.

CUMMINGS, R., BROOKSHIRE, D., and SCHULZE, W. (1986) (eds.),
   Valuing Environmental Goods. An Assessment of the Contingent Valuation Method, Totowa: Rowman and Allanheld.

DESVOUSGES, W.H., JOHNSON, F.R., and BANZHAF, H.S. (1998),
   Environmental Policy with Limited Information. Principles and Applications of the Transfer Method, Cheltenham, Edward Elgar.

EUROPEAN COMMISSION (1998),
   "State of Application of Regulation (EEC) No. 2078/92: Evaluation of Agri-Environment Programmes", Brussels, DG VI, Commission Working Document [VI/7655/98], available online on: *http//www.europa.eu.int/comm./dg06/envir/programs/index_en.htm*.

HANEMANN, W. (1984),
   "Welfare Evaluations in Contingent Valuation Experiments with Discrete Responses", in *American Journal of Agricultural Economics*, No. 66(3), pp. 332-341.

HANEMANN, W.M. and KANNINEN, B.J. (1998),
   "The Statistical Analysis of Discrete-Response Contingent Valuation Data", in Bateman, I.J. and Willis, K.G. (eds.): *Contingent Valuation of Environmental Preferences: Assessing Theory and Practice in the USA, Europe and Developing Countries*, Oxford, Oxford University Press.

HANLEY, N. and RUFFELL, R. (1993),
   "The Contingent Valuation of Forest Characteristics: Two Experiments", in *Journal of Agricultural Economics*, No. 44(2), pp. 218-229.

HAUSMAN, J. (1981),
   Exact Consumer's Surplus and Deadweight Loss, in *The American Economic Review*, No. 71, pp. 662-676.

HOEHN, J. (1991),
   "Valuing the Multidimensional Impacts of Environmental Policy: Theory and Methods", in *American Journal of Agricultural Economics*, No. 73, pp. 289-299.

HOEHN, J. and LOOMIS, J. (1993),
   "Substitution Effects in the Valuation of Multiple Environmental Programs", in *Journal of Environmental Economics and Management*, No. 25(1), pp. 56-75.

HOEHN, J. and RANDALL, A. (1989),
   "Too Many Proposals Pass the Benefit Cost Test", in *American Economic Review*, No. 79(3), pp. 544-551.

JOHANSSON, Per-Olov (1987),
   The Economic Theory and Measurement of Environmental Benefits, Cambridge, Cambridge University Press.

JUST, R., HUETH, D., and SCHMITZ, A. (1982),
   Applied Welfare Economics and Public Policy, Englewood Cliffs, N.J., Prentice-Hall.

KAHN, James R., STEWART, Steven and O'NEILL, Robert (1999),
   "Stated Preference Approaches to the Measurement of the Value of Biodiversity", paper presented at the OECD Workshop on "Benefit Valuation of Biodiversity Resources" OECD, Paris, 18-19 October 1999.

LAREAU, T.J. and RAE, D.A. (1989),
   "Valuing WTP for Diesel Odour Reductions: An Application of Contingent Ranking Technique", in *Southern Economic Journal*, No. 55, pp. 728-742.

MADUREIRA, Lívia (2000),
PhD Thesis to be submitted to the Universidade de Trás-os-Montes e Alto Douro (part of the results are available, in Portuguese, as a research report to the Portuguese Ministry of Agriculture).

McCONNELL, K. (1990),
"Models for Referendum Data: the Structure of Discrete Choice Models for Contingent Valuation", in *Journal of Environmental Economics and Management*, No. 18, pp. 19-34.

McCONNELL, K. (1992),
"Model Building and Judgement: Implications for Benefit Transfers with Travel Cost Models", in *Water Resources Research*, No. 28, pp. 695-700.

McFADDEN, D. (1974),
"Conditional Logit Analysis of Qualitative Choice Behaviour", in Zarembka, P. (ed.): *Frontiers in Econometrics*, New York: Academic Press, pp. 105-142.

MITCHELL, R. and CARSON, R. (1989),
Using Surveys to Value Public Goods: the Contingent Valuation Method, Washington, DC, Resources for the Future.

OECD (1999a),
Cultivating Rural Amenities: An Economic Development Perspective, Organisation for Economic Co-operation and Development, Paris.

OECD (1999b),
Environmental Indicators for Agriculture. Volume 1. Concepts and Framework, Organisation for Economic Co-operation and Development, Paris.

OECD (1999c),
Environmental Indicators for Agriculture. Volume 2. Issues and Design (The York Workshop), Organisation for Economic Co-operation and Development, Paris.

OECD (2000a),
"Production, Externality and Public Good Aspects of Multifunctionality: Introduction", document [COM/AGR/APM/TD/WP(2000)3/PART1], Organisation for Economic Co-operation and Development, Paris.

OECD (2000b),
"Externality and Public Good Aspects of Multifunctionality", document [COM/AGR/APM/TD/WP(2000)3/PART3], Organisation for Economic Co-operation and Development, Paris.

OECD (2000c),
Production, Externality and Public Good Aspects of Multifunctionality: Annexes [COM/AGR/APM/TD/ WP(2000)3/PART5].

OECD (Forthcoming),
Environmental Indicators for Agriculture. Volume 3. Methods and Results, (The Stocktaking Report), Organisation for Economic Co-operation and Development, Paris.

PALMQUIST, Raymond B. (1991),
"Hedonic Methods", in Braden, J. and Kolstad, C. (eds.): *Measuring the Demand for Environmental Quality*, Amsterdam, North Holland, pp. 77-120.

PEARCE, David (1999),
"Valuing Biological Diversity: Issues and Overview", paper presented at the OECD Workshop on "Benefit Valuation of Biodiversity Resources", OECD, Paris, 18-19 October 1999.

RANDALL, A. (1991),

"Total and Nonuse Values", in Braden, J. and Kolstad, C. (eds.): *Measuring the Demand for Environmental Quality*, Amsterdam, North Holland, pp. 303-321.

SANTOS, José Manuel L. (1998),

The Economic Valuation of Landscape Change. Theory and Policies for Land Use and Conservation, Cheltenham, Edward Elgar.

SANTOS, José Manuel L. (1998),

"Evaluating Multidimensional Biodiversity Policy: What Can We Learn from Contingent Valuation Studies of Biological Resources in the Context of Rural Amenities?", paper presented at the OECD Workshop on "Benefit Valuation of Biodiversity Resources", OECD, Paris, 18-19 October 1999.

SMITH, V. Kerry (1992),

"On Separating Defensible Benefit Transfers from "Smoke and Mirrors"", in *Water Resources Research*, No. 28, pp. 685-694.

SMITH, V. Kerry (1993),

"Nonmarket Valuation of Environmental Resources: An Interpretative Appraisal", in *Land Economics*, No. 69(1), pp. 1-26.

VAUGHAN, W., and RUSSELL, C. (1982),

"Valuing a Fishing Day: An Application of a Systematic Varying Parameter Model", in *Land Economics*, No. 58, pp. 450-463.

WARD, Frank A. and BEAL, Diana (2000),

Valuing Nature with Travel Cost Models, Cheltenham, Edward Elgar.

WILLIG, R. (1976),

"Consumer's Surplus without Apology", in *The American Economic Review*, No. 66, pp 589-597.

WILLIS, Ken and GARROD, Guy (1994),

"The Ultimate Test: Measuring the Benefits of ESAs", in Whitby, Martin (ed.): *Incentives for Countryside Management: The Case of Environmentally Sensitive Areas*, Wallingford, UK, CAB International, pp. 179-217.

Comments by Peter Berkowitz, European Commission, DG Agriculture

Let me start by saying that within the assumption-framework set by the author, he achieves quite elegantly his objective of providing a contingent valuation methodology for multiple non-commodity outputs. In this respect it places contingent valuation clearly in the centre of the debate about agri-environmental policy.

One area of particular interest and innovation relates to the results on valuing bundled outputs and independent valuation and summation. Substitution and complementarity in consumption of non-commodity outputs is a particularly interesting phenomenon, since it could potentially reflect two processes: the first is the interaction between natural features and the consumer's perception and the underlying factors organising this relationship. The second is the systematic interaction between different elements of agri-ecosystems. In both cases, we return to the notion of landscape as an organising factor in the relationship of a cluster of environmental characteristics. The multiple output valuation technique could provide us a way of better understanding processes on the demand side as regards agri-ecosystems.

I have little to say as regards the technical argumentation that is quite convincing within the framework of assumptions. My comments will focus mainly on these assumptions and the implications with respect to the practical application of the method.

1. Specification of Outputs

The first central problem relates to what might be characterised as the specification of non-commodity outputs. This, perhaps, more than questions of valuation is the key technical issue for the purpose of policy analysis in this field. To put it simply, before we seek to determine the amenity value of changes brought about by the Uruguay round we need to be able to adequately specify both the commodity and non-commodity impacts of the policy shift as well as the counterfactual situation. In the first instance, the question in hand is technical or even physical and not economic.

In the context of policy analysis we run quite quickly into the limiting factor of absence of knowledge. It is often tempting in the context of Contingent Valuation to shift the burden of filling in the gaps to the consumer. Furthermore, concerns about bias and legitimacy in the framing of scenarios are likely to be amplified in this context. The question of definition of non-commodity outputs is therefore not a question of "technical refinement" as suggested by the author in the text, but a fundamental limiting factor of the scope of the method. We should therefore not underestimate the value of natural science in specifying what is actually happening.

The author is fully correct where he highlights the importance of the question "what are we valuing?" But this question cannot be answered if we do not have objective information about the physical nature of the phenomena we are measuring.

The author's criticism relating to behavioural data that it needs to be interpreted to reveal preferences and values, can be equally applied to hypothetical data. This shifts the exercise of preference interpretation to the consumer. The extent to which contingent valuation merely shifts unanswerable questions from the analyst to the consumer should not be underestimated. Perhaps worse, in processing the data collected the analyst is unlikely to be aware of the underlying assumptions of consumers and therefore will impose his or her own, creating potential distortions. (The process will generate point elasticities but not the whole demand curve).

2. Assumption of pure publicness

The paper clearly limits itself to pure public goods since there are problems of aggregation linked to semi-public goods. However, the paper focuses largely on locally consumable non-commodity outputs linked to site visits. In terms of data collection this has clear advantages, as well as in the definition of the consumption function. Yet this is clearly an area where there is rivalry of consumption and consequently congestion effects. We should really ask, in the context of the policy questions that interest us, how many of the non-commodity outputs are really pure public goods? The issue here is the degree of publicness. This will have central implications for the aggregation of values and the appropriate attribution of quantities.

3. Questions of scale

This problem is compounded by the statement that scale does not necessarily matter for consumption. This doesn't make sense when questions of access and congestion come into play. Furthermore, scale is important as regards consumption in as much as strategic behaviour on the part of consumers depends on their proximity to the good. Even if there is no rivalry of consumption, there is a possibility of collective action problems particularly where taxes are concerned, as distant users defect. And of course, option value must be dealt with.

4. Transaction costs and alternatives

The suggestion that only marketisation or valuation offer solutions to avoiding policy failure is overstated. The most frequently used mechanism, at least in a European context, is not considered, that is to say democratic decision-making leading to setting of targets. This may involve a range of other approaches such as top-down target setting, risk assessment, output benchmarking or simply local politics. Since all methods are conducted in the context of imperfect information, real life budgetary constraints and all types of bias, their relative merits compared to contingent valuation are an empirical and not a theoretical question.

The author suggests that increased income, which is more than compliance cost, implies policy rents and these are by definition overcompensation. The basis for this somewhat pejorative term is unclear. In general, producer rents exist for every provider down to the marginal one. The existence of producer rents is common to markets. They pose not only no efficiency problems, but provide also incentives for technical progress. Furthermore, unless each farm is individually appraised, there will always be some producer rents. This would imply tremendous transaction costs. This problem is accentuated, particularly in the contest of bidding systems by the lack of homogeneity of non-market outputs.

5. Conclusion

There would appear to be significant difficulties and restrictions on the method:

- restriction to pure public goods, with no treatment of congestion effects and various degrees of publicness;
- dependence on other analytical frameworks for proper definition of what is to be valued;
- potentially high transaction costs in application, compared to other approaches;
- problems of bias, interpretation and legitimacy;
- inadequate treatment of scale effects;
- understanding of demand interactions.

It is difficult to say, as the author does, that available non-market valuation techniques are completely up to the task of unbiased valuation required by several policy uses: evaluating policies, investment projects, agri-environmental schemes, rural development programmes, conservation and providing management information.

He nevertheless recognises some of these problems in conclusion: complexity of detailed considerations, identification of relevant non-commodity outputs, need for perception-consistent definitions, the scale of aggregate values generated.

In a European perspective, contingent valuation cannot replace informed public debate at a range of levels and sound scientific analysis of agri-ecosystems. It is nevertheless an interesting complementary tool that merits further development, particularly as regards the examination of demand interactions.

**Comments by Gonzague Pillet, University Of Fribourg, Fribourg, And Ecosys®
Inc., Geneva**

**Emternalities Vs. Externalities:
Calling attention to the multiple non-commodity inputs question**

Summary

Lima e Santos' paper addresses the nature of the valuation problem in the context of joint, multiple, commodity and non-commodity, outputs from agriculture. The objective is to "design policies for welfare-increasing moves of that multiple-output bundle, or even to select a welfare-maximising bundle". This discussion paper is intended at showing that *a*) multiple, commodity and non-commodity, inputs to agriculture matter; *b*) production of multiple outputs from agriculture is jointed to multiple inputs to agriculture; *c*) empirical evidence does exist with respect to the valuation of multiple, commodity and non-commodity, inputs to agro-processes. While multiple non-commodity *outputs* are *externalities*, multiple non-commodity *inputs* are *emternalities*. In conclusion, designing policies disregarding multiple-input bundles or taking them into account as fixed may lead to further policy failures.

1. Issue and policy context

From the perspective of economic accounting, the size of agriculture is conceptually defined to include only goods (food and fibre) and services ("agri-tourism") that are bought and sold in market transactions (with few exceptions). Economic accounts generally *"record and measure activities that pass through the marketplace, while most of the activities that raise environmental concerns – from air pollution to appreciation of pristine wildernesses – take place outside the market"*. (Nordhaus and Kokkelenberg, 1999, p. 19). As a consequence, an important part of the very picture of agriculture is missing if not only multiple effects of agriculture on society and the environment but also natural inputs to agriculture are omitted in retaining conventional market-based accounts for agriculture. These omissions impact on policies in as much as by underestimating valuable nonmarket components in decision making processes, they overstate the role of market goods and services in economic welfare, providing misleading measures with respect to the overall performance of agriculture, especially in relation with sustainability concerns.

Expanding conventional accounts and standard valuation models by expanding their boundaries to include measures of these "missing residuals" provides a better estimate of the seize, functions, and growth of agriculture in relation with society and the environment. In this respect, the output side is concerned with the valuation of *externalities* and public-good non-commodity outputs from agriculture while the input side is concerned with the valuation of *emternalities* and public-good non-commodity inputs to agro-processes. Valuing multiple, non-commodity, joint inputs to agriculture constitutes the purpose of this discussion paper.

2. Emternalities vs. externalities

Emternalities are a semi counterpart to economic *externalities*. They represent and are a measure of the "environmental fraction" that goes through economic processes, is embodied in multiple commodity and non-commodity outputs, but which is not captured by commercial markets. In contrast, *externalities* stand for and dimension non-commodity outputs that spill over commercial markets.

Because commercial markets do not capture emternalities, neither prices nor economic values are available. Analysis of the agricultural sector in terms of emternalities – in supplement to that of externalities – is a significant issue because the free environmental fraction embodied in agro-products (commodity and non-commodity outputs) might prove significant, and the environmental pressure of the sector is particularly obvious.

An overview of emternalities and externalities is given in Figure 2 below. The particular prefix "em-" aims at emphasising the "into" attribute of emternalities (as a variant of "en-", *em-* refers to "put into").

Figure 2. **Emternalities vs. externalities**

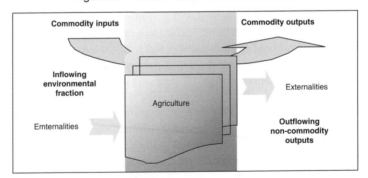

3. Joint input and output bundles

A further analytical issue lies in joining multiple, commodity and non-commodity, input and output bundles. The point is that externalities should be assessed as joint products or services, *i.e.*, as a special case of joint production (Buchanan, 1966). A general externalities joint production model can be used that shows joint inputs as $-q_{hj}(h{\neq}i)$ using a production function for j as the one that follows (Pillet, 1980):

F_{ij} $(q_{ij},\ Z_{kv},\ -q_{ij},\ -q_{hj}) = 0$, and $F_{rj}(Z_{jv},\ -q_{hj}) = 0$ where $r = v{+}1 = 2, ...,R;\ q_{ij} = $ commercial outputs vector of j; Z_{kv} and Z_{jv} being matrices of externalities (received by firm j/produced by firm j).

4. Some Empirical Evidence on the Emternality Side

Emternalities are evaluated in energy, eMergy and then GDP\$-value terms, eMergy being a quantitative tool for valuing natural ecosystems interacting with economic systems. The economic system itself is considered an ecosystem using free environmental flows as non-commodity inputs into agricultural production and use. Several studies are available (see References). The table below shows results as emternality fractions into multiple inputs to agro-processes (externality ratios) for different agro-processes and regions world-wide. These values matter.

Table 3.   **Empirical valuation of emternalities in different agro-processes and regions**

Region	Agro-processes	Emternality ratios
Geneva, Switzerland	Vineyard cultivation	19.3%
Florida	Tomato	5.8%
	Corn Grain	55.4%
	Sugarcane	34.1%
Takamatsu, Japan	Rice	13.1%

Source: Pillet *et al.*, forthcoming (original analyses by G. Pillet, S. Brandt-Williams and G. Pillet and T. Murota).

References

BRANDT-WILLIAMS, S. and BROWN, M.T. (forthcoming),
EMergy as a Market Trend Indicator: Examples in Florida Agriculture.

BUCHANAN, J.M. (1966),
"Joint Supply: Externality and Optimality", in Economica.

ECOSYS® (2000),
Appréciation quantitative des externalités de l'agriculture suisse/Externalities in Swiss Agriculture: An Assessment, Swiss Federal Office of Agriculture, Berne, 162 pages + 62 pages Annexes.

LAN, S., ODUM, H.T. and LIU, X. (1998),
"Energy flows and Emergy Analysis of the Agroecosystems of China", in Ecologic Science No. 17(1).

NORDHAUS, W.D. and KOKKELENBERG, E.C. (Eds.) (1999),
Nature's Numbers: Expanding the US National Economic Accounts to Include the Environment, National Research Council, National Academy Press, Washington, DC, 250 pages.

PILLET, G. (1987),
"Case Study of the Role of Environment as an Energy Externality in Geneva Vineyard Cultivation and Wine Production", in Environmental Conservation No. 14(1), pp. 53-58.

PILLET, G. (1980),
"Joint Production of External Diseconomies", in Economie appliquée No. 33(3-4), pp. 651-62.

PILLET, G., ZINGG, N., MARADAN, D. and BRANDT-WILLIAMS, S. (forthcoming),
Emternalities: Theory and Assessment.

PILLET, G. and MUROTA, T. (1988, rev. 1990),
"Shadow-Pricing the Role of Environment as an Energy Externality in Geneva's Vineyard and Wine, Louisiana Sugar-Cane-Alcohol, and Japanese Sake", unpublished.

ULGIATI, S., ODUM, H.T. and BASTIANONI, S. (1992),
"EMergy Analysis of Italian Agricultural System. The Role of Energy Quality and Environmental Inputs", in Proceeding of the Second International Workshop on Ecological Physical Chemistry, Milan, Italy, 25-29 May 1992, Trends in Ecological Physical Chemistry pp. 187-215.

Comments by Mikitaro Shobayashi, Agriculture Directorate, OECD

I provided the participants with the latest information on the progress of the OECD's work on multifunctionality, placing special emphasis on the linkage between demand measurement issues regarding non-commodity outputs and our further work on multifunctionality. In this context, I appreciated the important and pioneering work by Prof. Santos on analysing demand interactions between public goods. This would be, as I explain below, essential for policy discussions on multi-functionality at a later stage.

The work on multifunctionality was divided into three stages, which are: 1) conceptual analysis; 2) demand measurement issues; and 3) policy discussions. The OECD Secretariat prepared five sets of documents for the first stage of the work, focusing on production, externality and public good aspects of multifunction-ality. These documents were well received by the Agricultural Committee, and will be revised to incorporate comments from OECD Member countries. The revised versions will be submitted to the September APM/JWP meeting for possible declas-sification. This workshop constitutes part of the second stage of the work. The OECD Secretariat will assess whether there could be a need for further work on demand measurement, which will also be discussed at the September APM/JWP meeting.

In the conceptual analysis, an analytical framework was proposed as the basis for the future policy discussions. This analytical framework is represented by three sequential questions. Only in situations where the answer to all these questions is "yes", could there be conflicts between domestic and international policy objectives. These three questions are:

- Is there a strong degree of jointness between commodity and non-commodity outputs that can not be altered, for example, by changes in farming practices and technologies?

- If so, is there some market failure associated with the non-commodity outputs?

- If so, have non-governmental options (such as market creation or voluntary provision) been clearly ruled out as the most efficient strategy?

Demand measurement issues have emerged as very important ones, because our capacity to measure demand affects how we answer these questions. More specifically, the second and the third questions are directly linked with demand measurement of non-commodity outputs.

Regarding the second question, the conceptual documents examined exactly when and how markets fail due to externalities, and showed that non-commodity outputs that constitute positive externalities do not necessarily cause market failure. Theoretically, a positive externality causes market failure because producers do not take the benefits of the externality to society into account and therefore under provide the good that generates it. In reality, market failure is more complicated, depending on how the demand for the externality is distributed. For example, suppose that a certain externality is produced in some fixed proportion to commodity output irrespective of the location or cost of that commodity production, but that demand is fully met by the amount that is produced jointly by the lowest cost producers. In this case, no market failure occurs because the quantity of the externality that society demands can be fully met without an increase in the supply of the commodity (see Figure 3 below).

Figure 3. **Positive externalities where government intervention is unnecessary**

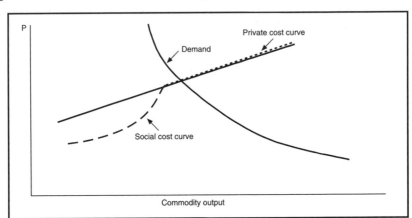

Regarding the third question, even if some non-commodity outputs are positive externalities that cause market failures, government intervention is not necessarily the best option. There are various ways to narrow the gap between social and private costs, depending on the specific public good characteristics of these non-commodity outputs. Many options would require no government intervention or very limited intervention, *e.g.*, to facilitate market creation. A detailed classification of public goods is therefore needed. Otherwise there is a risk that goods as disparate as toll roads, national defence, community-owned natural resources, municipal fire protection services and fisheries would be discussed together without acknowledgement of the extent to which their different public good characteristics should lead to different policy conclusions.

Possible policy failures associated with incorrect estimation of the demand for public goods strengthen the need for a detailed classification of public goods. If such errors are likely, provision arrangements that do not require demand estimation, including market provision, might be preferable to government provision, even if these alternative arrangements could also cause inefficiency (*i.e.*, underprovision).

Measuring demand for multiple non-commodity outputs would be much more complicated when there are some consumption relationships (or "demand interactions" as Prof. Santos defined) among these non-commodity outputs. As the paper of Prof. Santos clearly indicated, there could be risks of overestimating demand for multiple non-commodity outputs by adding up demand for each individual non-commodity output if there are substitution relationships between some of these non-commodity outputs. There could be consumption relationships between non-commodity outputs and negative externalities, which also need to be well addressed in the policy discussions.

We feel that understanding consumption relationships is important when discussing institutional arrangements, as well as when trying to measure demand for multiple non-commodity outputs. For example, even a pure public good could be provided through voluntary provision or the market if it has a complementary consumption relationship with an impure public good or a private good.

Chapter 4

Valuation by Whom, for Whom? Questions of Legitimacy

by
John Foster and Robin Grove-White
Centre for the Study of Environmental Change, Lancaster University, UK

Over the past decade and a half, the growing official interest in contingent valuation and other methods of representing environmental values in surrogate economic terms has been paralleled by strengthening criticism of assumptions underpinning the methods by philosophers, geographers and sociologists (Sagoff, 1988; Foster, 1997).

In this paper, we point first to some features of the forms that controversy has taken – before moving to discuss how the concept of valuation itself may need now to be approached more systematically under contemporary political conditions.

1. Some problems

Recent historical experience suggests that, in the UK at least, economic valuation methods applied to environmental goods have been developed overwhelmingly with the assumed needs of public administration in mind. The Third London Airport controversy of the early 1970s, the national motorways programme, the Ministry of Agriculture's land drainage programmes – these proved the initial forcing grounds for the development of such valuation methods. In the early 1990s, with the heightening profile of environmental issues in public policy, a succession of initiatives ensued, by both government departments and agencies and research funding councils, aimed at a heightened role for contingent valuation (CV) and similar techniques in policy development (*e.g.*, Doe, 1992).

It is not hard to understand the apparent merits of the methods when seen from a bureaucratic perspective. Surrogate valuation techniques like CV purport to capture and represent "objectively" the public values in play with respect to particular phenomena. Through standardised questionnaires, leading to numerical distillations of people's "preferences" (whether inferred, or directly expressed), such exercises appear to render tractable the messy world of public values, so that the findings can be reflected in public decisions balancing costs and benefits. That at least has been the promise.

However, a body of recent research experience gives cause for doubts. Not only is there evidence that people whose responses have been incorporated into such surveys may feel misrepresented by them. But also, the results produced by the surveys depend fundamentally on the initial "framing" assumptions embodied within them – assumptions that tend to be taken for granted within the closed framework of technical specialists responsible for such exercises.

The cases mentioned immediately below illustrate some of what appears to be at stake. The insights they yield go with the grain of deeper normative criticisms (in for example Sagoff, 1988, and Foster, 1997) of the excessively atomised individualistic conception of the human subject implicit in neo-classical economics (and thus pervading CV and similar techniques). The implication, as we go on to argue, is an urgent need for a wider range of insights to be incorporated into the development of new valuation methods, if improved public legitimacy is to be secured.

1.1. Dungeness and "the public"

A qualitative study (Burgess *et al.*) funded by English Nature in 1996 conducted interviews with sample members of the public who had previously been part of a CV exercise at Dungeness, Kent. The study found that such people felt seriously misrepresented by the reductionist framings of the CV exercise and by the artificially quantified representations of their views and perspectives on personally and publicly significant issues.

The study points to the extent to which CV may involve an artificial recharacterisation of complex human processes of shared negotiation and judgement in simplistic "Procrustean" terms – even if, when actually surveyed in the context of such a CV exercise, people generally do not object explicitly at the time. It also underlines the extent to which, in purely human terms, people may tacitly resent the representation of personally important matters in such reductionist terms – with subsequent corrosive implications for public identification with official decisions.

CV "findings" are probably leading officials to assume a greater degree of public accord with their approaches than may in fact exist.

1.2. Different methods, different values

A four-nation, EU-funded study on "Social Processes for Environmental Valuation" (O'Connor *et al.*, 1998) undertook parallel CV and "Citizens Jury" exercises, with respect to a putative "Wet Fen" creation scheme in East Anglia.

The study found that these respective "value elicitation" exercises, involving members of local publics and stakeholder organisations in the "Wet Fens" area, produced strikingly different pictures of what was at stake, and of the sorts of outcomes that might be appropriate. Table 4 (below) summarises some of the key differences arising from the two methods.

This adds further weight to the suggestion that CV and similar techniques generate necessarily selective (and methodologically idiosyncratic) accounts of the values which may be in play in environmental issues. This is not to claim that other methods – Citizens' Juries, for example – may not have other limitations of their own. Rather, it highlights the dangers of assuming that CV, etc., offer privileged, and hence politically robust, access to public values, in the way that some advocates claim.

1.3. Southern Water and Kennet abstraction proposal

In a 1998 controversy about costs and benefits of a putative major ground-water abstraction programme in a sub-region of southern England, CV was used by the Environment Agency (ENDS) in an attempt to capture local people's feelings about the significance of the issues at stake. Controversy then arose because the Inspector evaluating the Agency's case judged that the geographical canvas of the CV exercise (and hence the numbers and types of individuals whose views had been sought) was too broad, and should therefore be narrowed. The result was to drastically reduce the apparent local environmental costs of the scheme – as a simple arithmetical consequence of a bureaucratic-political judgement about which views should or should not count. Again, the case provides graphic support for scepticism about the intellectual "independence" of CV judgements, and hence about their political efficacy in politically sensitive circumstances. The case has proved seminal for the Environment Agency, in creating awareness of the need for more sophisticated approaches to valuation overall.

1.4. Woodland recreation and Forestry Commission

Consultants for the Forestry Commission, a statutory body that is the UK's largest landowner, undertook a major assessment of the public recreational values of the Commission's forests in the mid-1990s (ERM). This was deemed necessary to assist the Commission in its negotiations with the Treasury, on the issue of "revenue foregone" (from "clear-fell" timber production, for instance), in order to enhance public recreational benefits.

The exercise included a major CV study, which generated monetary representations of public values *vis a vis* particular levels of potential recreational provision. However, it became clear to independent researchers monitoring the exercise in 'participant observation' mode (CSEC, 1998) that the CV generated numbers in

93

Table 4. **Contrasting features of Contingent Valuation (CVM) and Citizens' Juries
as methods for eliciting value statements**

Distinguishing features of the two methods	Contingent valuation (CVM)	Citizens' Jury (CJ)
1) **Presuppose quite different pictures of the human subject and of human rationality and motivation**	People are utility-maximisers; their "optimising" behaviour is based on preferences that are "given" from outside the calculation domain.	People have mixed motives; their values are often indeterminate, but answer to context, and may be rationally structured on the basis of principled reasoning.
2) **Engage the subject in different ways**	Subject is reactive, isolated, individual; views are private and not open to challenge; subject is confined to one role.	Subject is interactive group member; views are public and open to challenge, subject is able to try out different roles.
3) **Make different demands on the subject**	Practice of the subject's calculative faculties and of their prudence.	Practice of the subject's reasoning faculties, skills and virtues.
4) **Promulgate quite different views of how issues are, or should be, framed**	Question(s) decided by researchers.	Question(s) evolve through negotiation among stakeholders, jurors and researchers.
5) **Embody quite different views of the relation between citizen and policy-maker**	Citizen as "customer" whose preferences and values it is the role of the policy-maker to satisfy and accommodate; relationship of mutual benefit – policy-maker invulnerable.	Citizen as citizen to whom policy-maker devolves, and with whom he/she shares, responsibility for decision-making; relationship of trust – policy-maker vulnerable.
6) **Produce quite different outcomes**	Quantified intelligence about people's concerns, which can be used both to validate policy and to estimate likely compliance with policy.	Rarely quantified, often unclear and sometimes inconsistent intelligence which reveals how people understand the environmental issues which they face.
7) **Handle "information" in quite different ways**	"Information" is (largely) anonymous and unquestioned.	"Information" is owned, defended and contradicted.
8) **See knowledge in a different light**	What matter is how much information is provided.	What matter is how information is construed.
9) **Proceed according to different "rules"**	Methodology is sovereign, process is theory driven and circumscribed.	Methodology is fluid, process is creative, dynamic, open ended.
10) **Handle distributional issues differently**	Condones existing distributions of rights; silences some voices (protest bids, income effects); open to manipulation by researchers.	Can challenge existing distributions of rights; silences some voices; open to manipulation by participants.
11) **Are validated in different ways**	Validation through precedent, consistency with previous studies, convergence and methodological rigour.	Validation through argument and mutual acknowledgement among participants (stakeholders, jurors, researchers).
12) **Need different institutional structures for assimilation of "results"**	Digestible by bureaucratic and financial structures.	Can be indigestible to traditional bureaucratic and financial structures.
13) **Have different endpoints in view**	The point of the exercise is in the outcome.	The point of the exercise is as much in the process itself as in its outcome.
14) **Have contrasting political significance**	Fosters "customer" habits and a managerial society.	Fosters civic habits and democratic values.

Source: Holland, A., *Grove-White*, R., O'Neill, J., *Spash*, C. (1998): from Martin O'Connor *et al.* 'ed.): *Walking in the Garden(s) of Babylon:* "An Overview of the VALSE project", University of Versailles: C3ED.

question had always been envisaged by both the Forestry Commission and the Treasury as flexible negotiating counters in the subsequent bureaucratic negotiations, rather than as unambiguous algorithmic representations of value (as assumed in most conventional economic discussions of CV "applications"). The researchers concluded: "CV *outputs need thus to be seen as heuristic, contrived to focus attention on otherwise under-represented public values, rather than as direct "objective" decision aids"*.

These examples point to a range of ways in which recent surrogate economic representations of environmental values have been encountering difficulties in the UK – both intellectual difficulties, and problems of political acceptability and legitimacy. The philosophical and sociological critiques, which have begun to throw light on such difficulties, have highlighted assumptions at the heart of neo-classical economic approaches to value itself as of central significance.

This is not the place to pursue such more abstract critiques in fuller detail. Instead, in the second half of the paper, we move from the lessons of the recent past to a discussion of the potential place of economic methods within a richer understanding of environmental valuation more generally.

2. A fresh approach

There are now a variety of recognised methods for taking account of environmental values in policy – and decision-making – on a spectrum from quantitative/ decisionistic to qualitative / deliberative:

- CBA / CV for non-market values;
- risk assessment;
- life-cycle assessment;
- multi-criteria analysis;
- focus group discussion;
- stakeholder negotiation;
- consensus conferences;
- citizens' juries.

The focus of preoccupation has shifted somewhat in the UK since the late 80s/ early 90s, from the quantitative (especially economistic) methodologies to the more participative and deliberative modes. To some extent this is due to the change in the general political climate, though this is easy to overstate – the "performance indicator" culture, still very much with us, is thoroughly quantitative (Power, 1997).

As already noted, the quantitative, economistic approaches have attracted criticism at both methodological and conceptual levels. For example:

- *framing assumptions* are made in ways which can mean that one, sometimes contestable, problem definition is built into the approach;

95

- *representation of objects to be valued* as discrete and susceptible of being quantified over itself itself involves contestable key assumptions about how people can and should relate to the natural environment;

- *use of metrics* with the associated appearance of precision can mislead;

- *deciding in conditions of indeterminacy* can involve misrepresenting genuine ignorance as statistical uncertainty;

- *the role of experts* can become that of expropriators of value;

- *public understanding and acceptance* has often been jeopardised by insistence on a quantificational approach in the face of quite justified scepticism and alienation.

By the same token, the more deliberative (qualitative methods have their own problems (often corresponding versions of the same problems) though maybe not yet so thoroughly exposed. For example:

- *framing processes* lead to questions about who is setting the deliberative agenda and by what authority;

- *relations of expert to lay judgement* – it is often not clear how far these are advisory and how far stipulative;

- *representativeness* – if not statistical, then what?

- *open-endedness* prejudices the robustness and transferability of decisions;

- *tensions between process and outcome criteria* – just how important is democratic inclusiveness when the environment is at stake?

What is becoming clear as the pros and cons of these different approaches are argued over is that they may all be understood as different *social processes* of valuation – configuring the relations between policy-makers, experts and the public in different ways, deploying different kinds of assumption and achieving different kinds of resolution, and so favoured differently by different constituencies and variously compatible with varying institutional cultures. And to see the range of methods in this light is also to recognise inescapably that we are not talking about different ways of accessing something – people's environmental values, say, or their relevant preferences – which exist out there independently of the methods, waiting to be accessed. Rather, the different methods themselves are at least in part constitutive of the values – they change the qualities and combinations of what they engage with. The choice of how to access public environmental values isn't a *prelude* to policy choice, it is already a form of such choice.

So a crucial question for policy agencies is that regarding *appropriate* usage of what we might better call different *methods of evaluative engagement* than methods of valuation or value capture.

For instance, the UK Environment Agency has a statutory duty to take costs and benefits into account in valuing environmental goods:

"In carrying out all of its functions the Agency is required to protect or enhance the environment so that it contributes towards achieving sustainable development. In doing so, the Agency must...take into account the likely costs and benefits of its actions." (UK Environment Agency Environmental Strategy for the Millennium)

The Agency's approach to this duty is also signalled in the same document:

"We will develop and use methods to:

- *assess the most cost-effective solutions when the benefits have already been decided on other (e.g., statutory) grounds;*

- *assess likely costs and benefits when the choices can be clearly costed;*

- *assess options when some aspects can be costed while others cannot, by using multi-choice techniques; and*

- *resolve conflicts by building consensus where matters are complicated and views are varied and extreme."*

This approach seems to go a fair way towards acknowledging that taking costs and benefits into account can in fact describe a wide variety of processes of reflection, discussion and option assessment in preparation for a decision – identifying and weighing up pros and cons, the advantages and disadvantages of particular actions, the strengths and weaknesses of particular arguments – the whole process of casting all this up and *deciding* answering to what we call *cost-benefit synthesis*, without any necessary implication that the process could be resolved or even assisted by cost-benefit *analysis* – although no doubt in some cases it can. Again, the crucial questions pose institutions like the EA with the challenge of making some demanding discriminations. What methods *are* appropriate in what kinds of situations? Where *does* it make sense to quantify values? Where *can* the metric usefully be money? Where must the approach be non-quantitative? How far need such approaches seek to build consensus, and how far are they about challenging, diversifying, problematising our understanding of what's going on?

In looking at the idea of what's appropriate here we are not just concerned with pragmatic questions, with what works, what horses for which particular courses, but also trying to understand why. What features (of situations and methods) would these discriminations reflect? There will clearly be a multiplicity of relevant aspects here, including:

- the social relations, including the power relations involved;
- the extent to which the "object of valuation" is given from outside the process as clear, delimited, agreed;
- issues of institutional credibility and public trust;
- the extent to which relevant economic information is available.

But we suggest that these issues of choice of methods all in one way or another map on to a pretty basic contrast and inherent continuing tension between *modes of valuation* – what we will call *open* and *closed* valuation.

Open valuation is:

- *exploratory* – it can lead us beyond what we thought we knew and felt – can find out new and unexpected meanings;

- *relational* – it can involve substantial recasting of our sense of our relations to what we're valuing, of how we stand to it, and who *we* are in these relations;

- *constitutive* – to the extent that things are defined at least in part by the relations in which they stand, this is a process which tends always to re-shape and develop both valuer and valued.

(Hence its "openness": it's in principle an unending process, since every valuation leaves valuer and valued changed, in ways which must then be explored evaluatively again.)

Does all this sound unduly high-falutin' in relation to (say) determining river water quality objectives? Well, *prima facie* it might. But just think of all the roles of rivers, to stick with that example, in the lives of people and communities – their unique potency as visible symbols of natural heritage in permanent motion. And then there's the accumulating empirical evidence, some of it noted above – researchers at CSEC and colleagues elsewhere are finding in studies of what actually goes on in environmental valuation, of how people experience their engagement with environmental issues, that they *are* often exploring, unsure, sensing mystery; perceptions *do* change and develop as the process goes on – people do find out about themselves and the others with whom they are sharing the process, and often they do feel any curtailment or closure of the process as arbitrary.

Inevitably, however, decision-makers and regulatory bodies must move to such closure – must adopt methods of *closed* valuation. Such valuation is characteristically:

- *adjudicative* – it tries to reach a conclusion, to sum up;

- *reifying* – it is more concerned with values inhering in, or projected onto, objects of valuation than with valuation itself as a process of exploratory adjustment;

- *comparative* – it is concerned to balance different values against each other, from a position where we as valuers are *holding* the balance, and so external to it.

Two points about this distinction between open and closed valuation are especially relevant in this context.

In the first place, and fairly obviously, if one looks at the spectrum of valuation methods, it is clear that the more deliberative ones more readily accommodate the open dimension of valuation, while the more quantitative ones are better adapted to the operational needs of policy institutions for closed valuation (see *e.g.*, Table 4 below) – so much so indeed, that such institutions are often not able to recognise the more "open" aspects of evaluative engagement as relevant to their concerns.

But in the second place, it should also be clear that valuing features of the natural world in which we humans so problematically belong is a process in which the drive towards *open* valuation is particularly strong:

- we are dealing with significant non-human others, and explicit judgements of value about such others in the context of human management is a new thing;

- we are surrounded by a great big *whole*, any provisional demarcations within which to be made for valuation purposes (separating out this aspect of these experiences and calling it a landscape, for instance, or delimiting the scope of a river authority's remit) are so very plainly provisional;

- "nature" has become a focus and a symbol for the sense of awe, the nervousness of hubris, which still lurks unconquered at the roots of our moral experience.

Because we are increasingly, and for all the good practical reasons comprising the sustainability agenda, recognising the urgency of the kind of decisions for which we need closed valuation, these two points together suggest why the *tension* between open and closed valuation – which is probably a permanent and constitutive feature of valuation of anything important – is so much more marked here than in many other areas, and has become a particular difficulty for institutions with environmental policy responsibilities.

The key question for such institutions and agencies, we would suggest, is: how can they *recognise* this continuing tension, in the twin senses of:

- telling confidently and reliably when they are confronted in given kinds of situation by this tension and its consequences; and

- "recognising" it in the way states and governments recognise each other – acknowledging the legitimacy of the concerns and approaches constituting open valuation, establishing working relations with these concerns, accommodating them creatively in institutional decision-making?

This is a crucial contemporary challenge to our resources of social and institutional intelligence.

Comments by John A. Dixon, World Bank

The paper by Foster and Grove-White presented itself as a critique of conventional economic valuation but really only amplified points that experienced economists already accept. There is no doubt that valuation of rural amenity values is difficult -- the goods in question are often public or quasi-public goods, property rights may be ill defined, and there are usually few effective markets for the provision of these services.

Economists, never shy to enter a new field, have applied a number of the valuation techniques in their "toolbox" to these issues. In particular, there is the fairly common use of various Contingent Valuation approaches (stated preferences approaches) to estimate the willingness-to-pay (WTP) or the willingness-to-accept (WTAC) for different quantities of rural amenity services. (The correct measure depends on the initial assignment of property rights: if one is being asked to give up/ lose something for which one has a *de fact* or *de jure* property right, the correct measure is WTAC; in the other case, an addition to what one has/ enjoys at present, the correct measure is WTP.)

The paper is critical of the results of several studies (largely of the WTP variety) that were carried out in England. In ex-post surveys with those initially surveyed the authors reported that the respondents were unhappy with the questions asked and the types of answers that they provided. This is a valid criticism, but valid for the studies, not the discipline of economic analysis. In fact, the solution proposed by the authors, Citizen's Juries, is precisely the sort of pre-survey testing of "focus groups" that should be done by an economist doing any CV study. Thus, the criticism of the discipline is unjustified, and their proposed solution is merely the first step in eliciting information that can then be used for policy analysis.

In fact, the Citizen's Jury approach has a major flaw: by not imposing any budget constraint or sense of "cost" for the actions that it considers, it is quite likely to give misleading results. Everyone wants a cleaner environment, more open space, fewer intrusions – it is just that there are costs to providing these services and there's the rub!

The real problem is that there are REAL costs associated with various types of rural amenity values, and those being asked to provide them often either demand compensation or are unwilling to forgo various development options. Hence the very important role for quantitative economic analysis. Government officials need to allocate scarce financial resources, and the UK environment authorities specifically require this type of analysis.

For valuation to be credible and accepted by both the public and the government, it is important that it has several characteristics: The good or service being valued must be clearly defined; the analysis must be transparent, with all of the assumptions made clearly specified, and the presentation of the results must be understandable. As mentioned earlier, it is important to understand the initial allocation of property rights so that the correct question – either WTP or WTAC – is asked.

Economists must also be open about explaining the levels of confidence that we normally have in different types of responses: when the good or service in question is what is called a "direct use value" (*e.g.*, one visits, consumes, or actively engages in the use of the service, such as by hiking across a rural landscape) then the level of confidence in the results from a well-done study are high. For tourism/recreation values, often measured by a form of either CV of travel cost analysis (a surrogate market technique), our level of confidence is medium. Confidence falls to low to medium when the extent of direct interaction with the landscape decreases or when the good or service in question has no easily observed market price (*e.g.*, the value of prevention of extinction).

Table 5. **Levels of confidence in estimates of the economic value of biodiversity**

Direct use values	High
Tourism/recreation	Medium
Ecosystem services	Low/Medium
Existence/option values (individual)	Medium
Existence/option values (genetic)	Very low-Medium

In all cases, the economic analysis has to be presented with the appropriate level of modesty and transparency (traits not shared by all economists, alas!!); and room made for other factors that may not have been included in the analysis and that may be very important. One thinks of specific cultural or religious aspects, or even national political concerns. The role of the economist is to provide information that can aid the decision making process, not to make the final decision based on the results of the analysis alone. Still, by quantifying where one can, the economist plays a very valuable role in this process, and forces others to enter the debate in a less emotional manner and move beyond saying that everything is "very" important, to trying to see where between zero and infinity these values actually lie.

Part 2

THE SUPPLY SIDE:
TRANSFORMING VALUES INTO REVENUES

Chapter 5

Current Policy Instruments: Rationale, Strengths and Weaknesses

by
Ian Hodge
Department of Land Economy, University of Cambridge

1. Who cares for amenities?

Rural amenities tend to have characteristics that mean that they are often not effectively provided through conventional markets. Externalities occur where the actions of one producer or consumer have direct consequences for the production opportunities or welfare of another producer or consumer and where these effects do not pass through a market. In the absence of a market, the decision-maker has no incentive to take these costs and benefits into account; farms causing pollution have no incentive to reduce it or farmers whose actions have the potential to create attractive landscapes have no incentives to create them. It is not always the case that because there is an externality that action should be taken. The pollution may have only trivial consequences and the cost of control may be high. The general point is that there is no market within which the production option is tested. And in the absence of this market test, possible changes in resource use that could increase the total level of welfare will be missed.

The primary reason for the persistence of this situation is the presence of transactions costs. These are the costs of obtaining information and of establishing and enforcing contracts. Transactions costs for rural amenities tend to be high due to the difficulties of measurement and their non-point origins. Rather than arising from a single point source, many amenities are associated with the general quality of the environment across large areas. Were transactions costs to be lower, the affected parties would be able to negotiate a solution under which both parties could gain. There is thus a role for government in either promoting the conditions under which such a test may be possible, by lowering or taking on transactions costs, or else to take more direct action.

Externalities relating to rural land uses are pervasive. Agricultural actives and other land uses are a source of both external costs and external benefits. Governments are intimately bound with all aspects of land use through the definition and enforcement of property rights, the prescription and enforcement of conditions for market transactions and through policies affecting all land use sectors. In these circumstances, a clear distinction between market and government failure becomes difficult to sustain.

Another, related limit to market activity arises because rural amenities exhibit what are often referred to as public good characteristics. They tend to be non-rival in that the availability of the good for consumption by one person is not decreased by consumption by another. They also tend to be non-excludable in that once provided, it is not possible to exclude people from enjoying their consumption. A typical example here would be an attractive landscape. In practice, most rural amenities have these characteristics to some degree, but they are rarely "pure" public goods. Non-rivalry occurs over some range of use levels. Public access to the countryside can be enjoyed by substantial numbers of people without affecting each others' enjoyment, but at some point congestion arises such that the quality of the recreation experience is reduced. Landscape can in principle be rendered excludable by setting up and enforcing boundaries around an area, but in practice the cost of so doing would exceed the revenue that might be obtained from the undertaking. Table 6 below shows a classification of rural amenities with different combinations of rivalry and excludability.

Table 6. **A classification of amenities**

	Rival	Non-rival (up to a point)
Excludable	Craft enterprises in Finland Coarseware pottery in Greece *Tanada* owner system Labelled products of French nature parks	Ruins and temples in Japan Canadian national parks Canadian historical sites
Non-excludable	"Everyman's right" to harvest natural products in Sweden	Austrian mountain farming French regional nature parks Terraced paddy field landscape in Japan Greek pottery villages

Source: OECD (1999).

Amenities may either originate from point or non-point sources. As has been more widely discussed with pollution, particular problems arise in the regulation of non-point sources in linking environmental impacts with actions by particular decision makers. The impacts are diffuse and difficult to measure and as a consequence, policies tend to concentrate on input use and production processes rather that more directly onto the environmental impacts themselves.

At first sight, the distinction between external costs on the one hand and external benefits and public goods on the other may appear straightforward. But in practice the distinction is less clear-cut. Typically, environmental impacts tend to be portrayed as external costs, with the implication that the solution should be sought through the application of the "Polluter Pays Principle" (PPP). But this represents an assumption with respect to the allocation of property rights. The decision as to whether any particular environmental impact is to be regarded as an external cost or benefit is essentially a political one. The application of public policy towards rural landowners has tended to accord to them considerable rights over the way in which the land may be used. However, as we note later, there is an increasing degree of regulation in the rural environment that is eroding the relatively privileged position of rural landowners.

The distinction can be portrayed in terms of a reference level with respect to environmental quality (Hodge, 1989; Hodge, 1994, OECD, 1999, Scheele, 1999). This level defines the particular allocation of individual property rights and hence the level of responsibility which landowners are required to adopt with regard to the wider implications of their choice of land use. Where landowners fail to achieve the reference level environmental quality, this will be regarded as an external cost. Where landowners achieve an environmental quality in excess of this level, they will be regarded as generating an external benefit. Some different types of amenity above and "disamenity" below the reference level are suggested in Figure 4 below.

Figure 4. **Amenities associated with rural land use**

Country services		
Landscape Biodiversity Ecosystem funtions Community support	**External benefits**	**Provider gets principle**
	Reference level for environmental quality	
Environmental damage		
Soil erosion Water pollution Pesticides in the environment Atmospheric emissions	**External costs: Polluter pays principle**	

Above the reference level, an alternative principle to the PPP may be applied. Beneficiaries may be expected to pay for the benefit provided; the "Beneficiary

Pays Principle" (BPP). In practice though, given the public good nature of the amenities provided, it is often not feasible to identify the beneficiaries and payments are often made by the government. This is thus a payment for the contribution which landowners make to environmental quality in excess of the reference level, reflecting a "Provider Gets Principle" (PGP) (OECD, 1994; OECD, 1996 and Hanley *et al.*, 1998). The PGP represents the critical principle in determining incentives to improve resource allocation. The BPP is thus more of an equity principle.

The reference level is not immutable. It is subject to movement in response to changes in political attitudes towards the rights and duties associated with land use and these are in turn influenced by a wide range of economic and social forces. Increasingly the reference level is coming to be defined more formally through various codes of practice. In some countries these have been written into legislation. In the UK they are voluntary, but the general principle is applied that in determining the levels of payments made in agri-environmental schemes compensation is not paid in respect of the costs of complying with these codes. The implication is then that when these codes are altered, effective shifts are being made in the character of property in rural land, *i.e.*, in the bundle of rights that define "ownership".

2. The amenity of nature or the nature of amenity

The relationship between the use of land and the amenities provided is not straightforward. It is generally conditioned by historical patterns of human influence. OECD (1999) suggests a categorisation of amenities based on different levels of human involvement: "almost intact nature" where amenity derives from a lack of human intervention, "interaction between man and nature" where rural areas have been transformed by human activities over long periods, and "man-made" where value stems from human constructions or traditions. In practice, some degree of human involvement will be almost inevitable. Few wilderness areas have been entirely free from human impact (*e.g.*, Budiansky, 1995) and most historical constructions and traditions in rural areas bear some influence from the local environment.

Agricultural activities cover a high proportion of the land in rural areas and so the relationship between agriculture and the environment is often central to the discussion of the provision of rural amenities. The figure below suggests a schematic illustration of a possible relationship through the use of a production possibility frontier (ppf). The figure indicates the potential combinations of agricultural output and environmental services that could be provided from an area of land. The shape of the ppf illustrates a common pattern where intensive agricultural production causes environmental damage, but where similarly, excessive extensification is also a source of environmental decline. Starting from a relatively high level of agricultural prices and intensive production, we may expect that a decline in prices and production intensity will first bring about an enhancement to environ-

Figure 5. **Environmental impacts
of alternative agricultural production intensities**

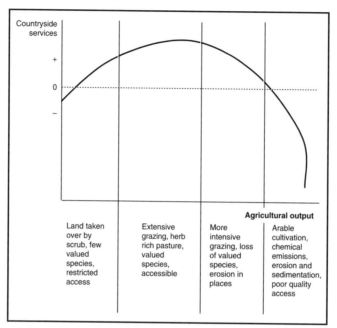

mental quality but that beyond some point further reductions will lead to a decline. For example, as the price paid for livestock products falls, grazing in marginal areas may become sufficiently extensive for undesirable scrub species to invade pastures that would otherwise support wildflowers. Similarly, if such farms enlarge and shed more labour in response to falling prices, their field boundaries will become increasingly redundant and fall into decline, as stock are left more to their own devices.

We can generalise this into two possible types of relationship between agriculture and the environment. The first of these, termed an 'input model', tends to be associated more particularly with a "New World" context and the second, an 'output model' with an 'Old World' context (Hodge, 2000).

2.1 The "input model" of environmental impact

The approach often adopted by North American and Australian commentators tends to view the impact of agriculture on the environment as an external cost associated with the intensity of input use (*e.g.*, Anderson, 1992; Dunn and Shortle, 1992; Zilberman, *et al.*, 1997). Water pollution provides a common example. Fertiliser and chemicals applied by farmers run off or are leached from farmland into aquifers and watercourses imposing external costs on water users and damaging ecosystems. Reductions in output prices lower the value of the marginal products of the inputs, lowering optimal use levels and hence lessening environmental damage.

This approach suggests that there is an inevitable and direct relationship between agricultural output prices and environmental quality. Provided that we accept certain basic premises from economics about the supply response in agriculture, a reduction in the level of price support inevitably leads to a reduced intensity of production and thus to an improvement in environmental quality. Reductions in other forms of support, such as area or headage payments, would also tend to reduce the incentives to keep land in potentially environmentally damaging production.

2.2. The "output model" of environmental impact

A rather different approach is more often stressed by European commentators. This emphasises marketed food and environmental quality as separate *products* of the land but which can be produced in varying combinations (*e.g.*, Buckwell, 1989; Russell, 1993 and Traill, 1988). In this case, the illustrative environmental impacts tend to focus on landscape and wildlife values. This model can have similar implications to the 'input model' where there is a competitive relationship between environment and agricultural production. This is reflected by the right hand side of Figure 5. A reduction in agricultural production would still be associated with an increase in environmental quality. However, the 'output model' more often assumes that, over certain levels and styles of production, particularly in respect of relatively extensive grazing systems, agricultural outputs and environment are complementary, as illustrated by the left hand side of Figure 5. This means that a reduction in agricultural prices and hence of production may lead to a *reduction* of environmental quality. Price reductions will alter the mix of environmental attributes associated with agricultural production and not be unambiguously beneficial. There is likely to be less chemical pollution, but also potentially fewer countryside services. Some recent research (*e.g.*, Doyle *et al.*, 1997; Potter *et al.*, 1999) has indeed suggested that the changes associated with liberalisation could be significant and damaging to landscapes and biodiversity in both marginal and mixed farming areas.

These two models would seem to have most direct relevance in different circumstances. The "input" model suggests an agriculture operated in opposition to the "natural" environment. In fact, the environment existing prior to the introduction of modern farming methods will usually already have been substantially modified by human activity and thus not appropriately be termed 'natural' (again, see *e.g.*, Budiansky, 1995). But the point is that what is regarded as the "natural" environment is *not a product* of this type of agricultural activity. In contrast, the "output" model is premised on agricultural systems that have co-evolved with the environment over substantial periods of time to the extent that there is a close interrelationship between the valued characteristics of the environment and certain attributes of the agricultural systems that are associated with them. These values may be lost either by excessive intensity of land use or by insufficient intensity or abandonment. Clearly there can be no guarantee that any particular level of agricultural prices determined in world markets will deliver the particular agricultural system required to generate the desired environmental values.

While this is characteristic of the "New World", "Old World"' divide, the linkages with particular places is not straightforward. (This will not be surprising given the Eurocentric judgement implicit in the "New"/"Old" terminology). For instance, there are landscapes in Europe where agricultural modernisation has effectively erased many of the valued environmental characteristics, such as in areas in East Anglia or the Paris basin. Conversely there are areas in the "New World" where particular land uses have themselves begun to produce valued landscapes, such as perhaps in New England. This thus does not support the idea that the "European" model should be regarded as consistently different from circumstances elsewhere, but it does indicate that history matters.

These assumed relationships between production and environmental variables may have parallels in the relationships between production and social or community variables. Traditional agricultural systems have also co-evolved with particular local communities and cultures. Thus the preservation of certain cultural and community values – such as their defining skills, knowledge and customs – may also depend upon the protection of the agricultural systems which have engendered them. Perhaps the most obvious example of this would be in many mountain communities where there are close links between collective agricultural activities and the organisation of local communities. Alternatively, in Britain an example would be crofting.

3. The scope and limits of valuation

The potential for the use of economic valuation techniques in setting standards and policies must vary considerably between different types of amenities. Some amenities, such as public access or the quality of the environment to those living within attractive landscapes may be amenable to valuation by being similar to payments already made for access to private parks or by being part of a value already paid for through the purchase of property. But it seems unlikely that we will ever be able to generate reliable and generally accepted valuations of many amenities, perhaps especially those associated with existence values or the extinction of species or the maintenance of cultural traditions. Thus, where particular processes provide a variety of different types of amenity, we should not expect to have a comprehensive valuation available.

In fact, in many contexts we may not have any form of quantification available at all to assist in policy making. Even simple measurement presents a considerable challenge to many types of amenity. In policy terms this is not unusual; similar types of problems are faced in decisions about defence or health expenditures. Can we value the contribution of a new submarine or an infantry battalion to the value of defence produced by the armed forces? I doubt it. Clearly though, judgements must be made about the importance of amenities in the determination of policy. This will have to rely on various indicators, such as the numbers of people affected, rarity or uniqueness of the assets involved, reproducibility, uncertainty and threats to preservation, the extent of public recognition, potential information value in the future, and so on.

Some evidence may be revealed by individual behaviour, especially in terms of willingness to pay for amenities where there are markets in operation, and willingness to make donations where there aren't. But such evidence requires careful interpretation. Some charismatic or emblematic species or artefacts may gain undue prominence in the media. Others assets may have values that are not widely recognised. Also free riding or strategic considerations may influence behaviour in real decision-making contexts, biasing the available evidence of underlying valuations. Nevertheless, in some circumstances, institutional changes may offer a means of enhancing the opportunities available for individuals to reveal the preferences through their actions and expenditures. This can provide information to policy-makers and should thus be considered as a factor in institutional design.

4. The range of policy instruments

Policy mechanisms may be developed to promote the provision of amenities in a number of different ways. These have different characteristics and different strengths and weaknesses. The aim must be to establish institutional arrangements that give all legitimate interests an opportunity to have an appropriate influence on resource allocation decisions and to establish mechanisms whereby funds may be transferred from beneficiaries, or their representatives, to those directly bearing the opportunity costs of the provision of amenities.

Figure 6 illustrates schematically the types of linkages that might be adopted in mechanisms for the provision of amenities. The top of the figure represents demand. The bottom the land owners who provide supply, thus bearing the opportunity costs of the provision of rural amenities. A variety of linkage mechanisms offer the means of relating demand and supply together. Private provision of point source amenities is often more straightforward and can often take place through the

Figure 6. **Alternative linkages in the provision of rural amenities**

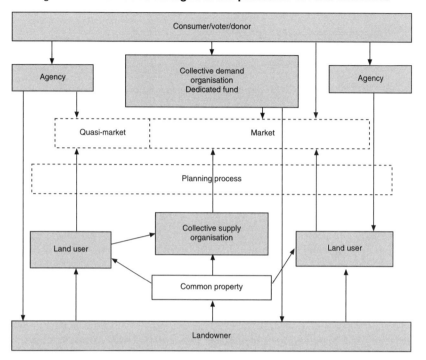

market. For instance, it is relatively easy to exclude people from ancient castles or chateaux and hence to charge for admission. However, even here there may be public good aspects of the conservation of ancient monuments and problems in generating sufficient funds from the market in order to provide proper maintenance. Governments may then provide support from public funds. Where non-point amenities are demanded, alternative arrangements are required. For instance, environmental contracts in agri-environmental policy are represented by a direct link between an agency and a land user or landowner. However, other arrangements may be more effective by revealing demand within a market context, by establishing incentives for landowners to co-ordinate their actions, or by reducing the requirements for public expenditure.

Policies may seek to alter the way in which property is owned or may operate through an intermediary organisation representing the collective demand of consumers or co-ordinating the actions of suppliers. Arrangements may establish incentives for the owners of assets to think entrepreneurially, to develop amenities without regular payments from government and without a continuing burden of transactions costs to the public sector. Opportunities may be developed for land-owners and others to make voluntary contributions for the benefit of environmental conservation.

4.1. Reducing policy disincentives

Before considering the positive contribution that public policy mechanisms can make to the provision of amenities, we should briefly review the potential arising from reforming existing arrangements, especially agricultural policies. Amongst a range of impacts, support for agriculture can increase the pressures on the environment leading to damage to the landscape, a loss of biodiversity and environmental pollution. This is clearly the case in the context of the "input" model discussed above. We can thus see the attractions of liberalising agricultural policy. Lower levels of agricultural support will reduce the incentives for more intensive production and relieve some of the pressure on the environment. Some advantages will have already been gained from reforms, which have shifted a significant element of support away from the maintenance of output prices towards direct payments to farmers. This will reduce the incentives to use higher levels of inputs because an increased proportion of agricultural support received is independent of the intensity of production; *i.e.*, it does not increase the return to input use at the margin.

However, the position is complex, as reflected in the "output" model, in that liberalisation can itself lead to environmental losses. In terms of the previous discussion, liberalisation can push intensive production back along the production possibility frontier raising environmental quality. But it cannot prevent agricultural production falling beyond the point where environmental quality declines due to excessive extensification. Some further environmental policies are required for this. A comprehensive liberalisation of agricultural policy will not be sufficient to deliver the standard of rural environmental quality that appears to be demanded.

4.2. Product definition and labelling

In some circumstances it is possible to redefine products in such a way as to stimulate the provision of countryside services. More careful definition of products and the provision of further information to consumers can enhance the return to production practices that are more consistent with the goals of conservation. This can stimulate markets for quality products that are associated with environmentally friendly agricultural practices, sometimes referred to as "niche markets" (OECD, 1995). Perhaps the most obvious examples are labelling for organic products or *Appellation d'Origine Contrôlée*. Consumers may be willing to pay a premium for these, either through a belief that the products are better or safer for the consumer than the alternatives or for less direct personal benefit as a contribution to environmental conservation.

Similar arguments may be applied to the development of commercial tourism based on the environmental quality of the local area. This may be supported by giving rights to operate tourist enterprises to local communities so that decisions on land use are made by the beneficiaries of tourist activities. Such changes would promote the diversification of farming systems towards a wider range of activities. But it may still fail to provide full market incentives for the production of amenities, rather it establishes markets for products with varying degrees of jointness in supply with them. Similarly, even within communities, those gaining commercial advantage from the presence of amenities will often not be the same as those who bear the opportunity cost of their provision. The scope in any particular situation will depend considerably on particular local circumstances. Hence the need for mechanisms that are responsive to the variability in local conditions.

4.3. Defining and rebundling property rights

Institutional changes may be able to promote market opportunities for the provision of countryside goods. For example, the definition and assignment of rights to non-timber forest products, such as access rights for sport and recreation or rights to harvest medicinal herbs or mushrooms have become significant sources of revenue in some forest areas (e.g., Mendelson, 1994; Merlo, 1995 and 1996). It may be possible to partition property rights to certain aspects of environmental quality and for interested individuals or groups to acquire conservation covenants over land use through the market (e.g., Hodge et al., 1993; Wiebe and Meinzen-Dick, 1998). This is a widely used mechanisms for the protection of farmland from development in the USA and it is also quite widely used by non-profit organisations for other uses (e.g., Endicott, 1993).

Merlo et al. (2000) have undertaken a systematic study of the increased marketability of goods provided by forests with public goods characteristics in four European countries. They describe transformation paths associated with institutional and management changes that in the great majority of cases involve increased rivalry and excludability. The authors conclude that recreational products that require structures and facilities additional to a high quality environment are more easily developed through the market, while those requiring the environment alone are less easily developed. However there is scope to capture at least some part of consumers' willingness to pay for the environment through product labelling, certification of environmentally based production processes and sponsorship. A wide variety of public and private organisations and partnerships have a role to play. The comment that the most challenging task for market based environmental policies is to establish linkages between those selling products associated with environmental quality and those responsible for environmental management.

4.4. *Leverage by demand groups*

A variety of private groups are established with a primary purpose of providing rural amenities. Such organisations are referred to as Conservation, Amenity and Recreation Trusts (CARTs) (Dwyer and Hodge, 1996). These are non profit-making organisations with the aim of generating wide public benefit through nature conservation and environmental improvement, provision of amenity and opportunities for public recreation and conservation of landscape heritage. CARTs represent demand for particular amenities provided at particular locations. They directly represent the interests of a demand group, often through a membership, and translate this into direct action for their provision. An illustration of the variety of types of CART found within the UK is shown in the box below.

Box 1. Variety of types of CART

Primary conservation CARTs – those for whom nature conservation is their main role, who buy or manage land as nature reserves.
e.g., The Wildlife Trusts, Royal Society for the Protection of Birds, Elmley Trust, Otter Trust, Butterfly Conservation, British Herpetological Society.

Primary heritage CARTs – those for whom the heritage value of land and landscapes are the main reason for acquiring and managing sites.
e.g., National Trust, Landmark Trust; Painshill Park Trust, Elan Valley Trust; Oxford Preservation Trust.

Primary amenity and recreation CARTs – groups for whom the ability to provide public recreation and amenity sites is the main reason for acquisition or management.
e.g., Buchan Countryside Group, Bryson House Better Belfast Project, Magog Trust, Groundwork Trusts, Shetland Amenity Trust, Shenley Park Trust.

Secondary CARTs – largely non-commercial groups whose objectives are mainly elsewhere but whose management of open land follows the same principles as CARTs.
e.g., Educational Trusts with environmental emphases [Commonwork, Bridge Trust, Camphill Trusts, Findhorn], Recreation groups with 'reserves' or conservation areas: [Mountaineering groups, Wildfowling societies, Railway/Canal Trusts].

The conservation organisation will have an incentive to seek out least cost ways of generating and protecting the conservation values under its particular circumstances. It will be prepared to trade off costs against conservation gains. Therefore such organisations will tend to act entrepreneurially, seeking new products and new methods of achieving conservation goals. They will respond to changes in relative prices and technology. Conservation organisations may also be more flexible and less bureaucratic than many government agencies given their generally smaller size and the lack of democratic accountability. They may be able to respond more rapidly to opportunities that arise, such as in purchasing significant conservation sites when they become available on the market. Such organisations often specialise in particular types of conservation, such as the protection of birds, or may focus their efforts within a particular area. In this way, although they may be relatively small organisations, they can build up a level of expertise within their own particular speciality. There are of course disadvantages. Small organisations may lack the relevant skills, may represent only a fringe interest, or may be 'captured' by minority interest groups amongst the membership in the face of the apathy of the majority. These risks are reduced by the need to raise funds and gain support from the general public but this itself implies that some such organisations will fail to survive, threatening the protection of the assets that they were established to conserve.

This type of policy is sometimes characterised in terms of the provision of club goods. But this is often not an accurate description. Bohman *et al.* (1999) comment that *"... multifunctional services do not necessarily require government provision. In some instances, club goods provide an alternative. Organizations like the Nature Conservancy and Ducks Unlimited, through admission and membership fees, finance the preservation of unique ecological niches"*. Club goods are defined by Bohman *et al.*, 1999) as goods that are relatively non-rival but excludable. But clearly many of the benefits produced by such organisations, especially ecological conservation, are not excludable. Rather, CARTS are raising funds from a variety of sources, including grants and tax relieves from government and private donations, in order to provide some relatively pure public goods (Dwyer and Hodge, 1996). The club goods model implies a market process driven by narrow self-interest. This does not effectively capture the ways in which such CARTs operate.

The CART model implies some change in the character of property owners. The state can promote the actions of such organisations, which have objectives more compatible with those of the state than is the case with the majority of private owners. This may be and indeed is done in terms of grants for the purchase of land, contributions towards labour costs and the tax relief generally available to charitable organisations. This suggests that the conservation organisation will require less detailed monitoring than a conventional landholder and that in the longer term it would be likely to develop more cost-effective methods of conservation management. In practice CART activities are significantly guided by the institutional and financial environment created by government and as such their role is better interpreted as "policy by intermediary" rather than "free market environmentalism".

4.5. Dedicated environmental funds

As noted by Merlo *et al.* (2000), those who benefit from market opportunities deriving from the presence of amenities are not the same as those whose decisions determine whether the amenity is provided and who face the opportunity cost of doing so. One mechanism for establishing such a linkage is through a dedicated fund. Funds may be established and operated either within the public or private sectors. They may raise funds from the public sector, such as a (hypothecated) tourist tax. In practice taxes may have an additional objective of limiting the impacts of tourism or recreation to limit the external costs of these activities, although there is no reason to believe that a single rate could meet funding raising and internalisation objectives simultaneously.

Donations may be solicited from those benefiting from the quality of the local environment on a voluntary basis, from the users directly, from firms whose business depends upon it in some way, or from people who have no direct connection with the area. Collection methods may range from simple collection boxes to more complex schemes such as linking payments to the use of particular credit cards. A few business chains have instituted a 'voluntary dollar' scheme, whereby customers are encouraged to make a voluntary donation that will be matched by the firm. Given the probable limits of voluntary donations, particularly because the public good nature of the benefits, more rigorous approaches are likely to be desirable.

The fund may be administered and used in many ways to promote local conservation. It may be operated by a local government or some non-governmental body. It may be used to finance environmental contracts or be directed through CARTs. Some illustrations of private dedicated environmental funds in the UK are shown in the box below. In practice these organisations become involved in a range of different types of activity in support of the environment so that the distinctions between the types of organisations are not always straightforward.

There is little information about the operation of these funds and a number of questions arise as to how they raise finance and how they are managed and controlled. However, where they operate at a local scale they are likely to be closely linked with local interests and local opportunities for the supply of amenities. Perhaps there is a greater concern here than there is with CARTs as to the accountability of decision-making where such funds operate outside of a formal government structure. Again, institutional design and public funding decisions will influence the way in which such funds operate and the resource allocations that arise from them.

4.6. Regulatory policies

Most countries have regulatory systems, especially land use planning mechanisms, which provide a basis upon which other mechanisms build. This underlying

---

Box 2.   Dedicated Environmental Funds in the UK

Local area funds

Amenity groups have developed to promote conservation of characteristic local environment. Sometimes action limited to lobbying, often to prevent local development. But also active in securing funds, providing advice and allocating grants for environmental improvements.

Friends of the Lake District established to protect the natural beauty of the Lake District and the surrounding countryside. Provides financial help for projects that will enhance the landscape and improve village amenities.

Environmental feature funds

Concentrate on specific components of the environment or types of habitat. Also generally have an association with a particular locality which acts as a focus for fundraising.

West Country Rivers Trust. Independent charity established in 1995 to protect and enhance rivers and streams in the west of England through working with landowners. Raise funds for specific projects. Concentrate on creating practical improvements and enlightening attitudes towards river rehabilitation.

Species funds

Established to promote the conservation of particular, usually emblematic, species seen to be at risk from environmental changes.

The Hawk Trust. Dedicated to the conservation and appreciation of birds of prey, in particular species native to UK. Policy is to promote enhancement of farmland, woodland and upland bird communities, working closely with landowners, farmers, foresters and gamekeepers.

---

framework is important in determining the role and character of other mechanisms. For instance, the town and country planning process in the UK effectively prevents urban development in the open countryside. This is a factor explaining the greater use of the acquisition of partial interests in land for the protection of agricultural land from urban development in the USA.

Over time there appears to have been some general tightening in the degree of regulation imposed over rural land uses. In the UK for instance, restrictions have been introduced over the building of intensive livestock units. Legislation was introduced in 1995 to protect hedges in England and Wales from deliberate removal. Although concerns remain among environmental groups about their effectiveness, these effectively extend a form of planning control over features on farm

119|

---

land. Legislation currently before Parliament proposes a shift in the balance of rights and responsibilities for the protection and management of Sites of Special Scientific Interest. Under this, conservation agencies would be empowered to refuse permission to landowners to undertake operations likely to damage without any requirement for the payment of compensation for the opportunities foregone. The balance in regulation of nitrate emissions has also shifted from compensation paid under Nitrate Sensitive Areas to regulations operated within Nitrate Sensitive Zones. And landowners have also lost the battle to prevent the government from introducing much wider rights of public access to the countryside. Similar changes are taking place in other countries, perhaps reflecting a weakening of the political influence of agricultural interests in the political process.

4.7. Government financial incentives

Payments may be made by government to landowners in order to promote the provision of amenities. Generally, we may assume that the closer the payment is tied to the provision of the service, the more effective is the mechanisms likely to be. But in practice, the difficulty of measurement and the uncertainty and time lag in the provision of the output mean that payments are more often made against input activities. Some payment mechanisms are particularly indirect, such as the provision of tax relief where the level of tax saving may bear little relationship to the social value of the output provided.

The predominant form of intervention with respect to agricultural land use has operated through voluntary environmental contracts established between a land-holder and a government agency under which the landholder agrees to follow a particular set of practices and not to undertake others. In return, the agency makes a payment, generally on an annual basis. Agreements accept that the farmer will continue in occupation of the land and assume that any specialist knowledge can be provided to farmers, either within or in association with the particular contracts on offer. The underlying premise to these contracts is that farmers hold the property rights to alter the environment and thus should be given positive incentives to change their practices, *i.e.*, that the Provider Gets Principle applies.

There are similarities between the policy mechanisms that are being developed in different countries, such as agri-environment policy under the Common Agricultural Policy in Europe (*e.g.*, Hanley *et al.*, 1999, Huylenbroeck and Whitby, 1999) and the Conservation Reserve Program (Feather *et al.*, 1999) and EQIP (Batie, 1999) in the USA. One difference in approaches has been the greater emphasis that has been given to payments for reductions in chemical emissions and soil erosion in the USA, impacts that might be regarded as below the reference level. While the balance appears to be shifting towards other environmental amenities, it probably reflects the "'New World" context and the increased relevance of the "input model" approach.

These schemes face a variety of challenges in identifying local preferences and in setting clear environmental objectives, in defining contracts to deliver them, in minimising excess payments to landowners, in enforcing compliance, in optimising transactions costs in targeting payments and providing information, in maintaining environmental benefits achieved over the longer term, and so on. Experience with such schemes is relatively short-lived and the problems are complex. Batie (1999) comments that the implementation of EQIP programme has left a gap between promise and performance but cautions against comparisons with an ideal that can never be realised in practice. It is necessary to make further progress, but we should not be too critical of what has been achieved so far.

4.8. Public ownership

A final alternative involves the public acquisition and management of land and other assets for the provision of countryside goods. The public ownership of land for the provision of amenities has survived the privatisations of the last twenty years and remains a common feature of national parks and nature reserves in many countries. This public ownership is not immune from the general problems of public sector management, the conservatism in decision making, political interference, the limited incentives for efficiency and so on. But there are contexts where private ownership is also problematic, such as where there are no revenue flows to be obtained from land management or where managers need immediate access to high quality research backup. Innovations in approaches to management and contracting may well reduce the range of contexts in which public ownership is seen as the appropriate solution, but nevertheless, some public land ownership may be expected to persist in the future.

5. The governance of rural amenities

We are currently responding to a major shift in the nature of rural areas, from a domination by concerns directly related to agricultural production towards one where the direct consumption of heritage and nature plays an increasingly dominant role. At the same time, the privately profitable forms of rural land management have come to produce lower standards of environmental quality. This requires a new focus on the conscious production of amenities for the enjoyment of the general public. The wide variety in the characteristics of rural amenities and the importance of the local historical, environmental and social context indicate the need for a complex mix of private and public mechanisms. Governments will be involved in many ways. This will include the provision of information, research and development, institutional change, the promotion of human capital and learning, direct funding and policy evaluation. In particular a number of aspects of rural amenity provision provide a significant challenge:

- Problems of measurement and valuation. While not unique to amenities, decisions have to be taken without the advantage of reliable measurements and valuation. Policy mechanisms will often have to be indirect, linked to proxy variables rather than the amenity itself.

- The influence of the local context and the demand for variety. Spatial variations in both demand and supply capacity imply that there will be significant variations in optimal outcomes across space. This implies a need for decision-making at a local level.

- Interrelationships between supply decisions across space. In a market, producers will respond to costs and prices and will thus have a clear incentive to co-ordinate their actions. In its absence, other institutions are required to promote co-ordination and collective action. The costs of co-ordination may be reduced through the maintenance or development of social capital.

These characteristics indicate a need for the development of new institutions at a local level. These may provide opportunities for individuals to reveal their demand for amenities through the payment of charges and donations. Arrangements are required to determine priorities at a local level; how to raise funds and how to spend them. Institutions can promote collective actions amongst groups of landowners for water level management, habitat protection or landscape creation. Within this there is a need for environmental and social entrepreneurship in identifying opportunities, controlling resources and taking risks. We can see evidence of all of these requirements being addressed in institutional innovations in a variety of locations and contexts, but the process of innovation, testing and refinement has a long way to go. Indeed given shifting goals and constraints, this is not a process that will ever be ended. But the process can be enhanced by developing clearer conceptual frameworks for analysis, by sharing information and experience and by evaluating the performance of alternative arrangements.

References

ABLER, D.G. and SHORTLE, J.S. (1992),
"Potential for environmental and agricultural policy linkages and reforms in the EC", in *American Journal of Agricultural Economics*, No. 74(3), pp. 775-781.

ANDERSON, K. (1992),
"Agricultural trade liberalisation and the environment: A global perspective", in *The World Economy*, No. 15(1), pp. 153-171.

BATIE, S. (1999),
"Green payments as foreshadowed by EQIP", Staff Paper 99-45, Department of Agricultural Economics, Michigan State University, East Lancing.

BOHMAN, M *et al.* (1999),
"The use and abuse of multifunctionality", Economic Research Service, US Department of Agriculture, Washington, DC.

BUCKWELL, A. (1989),
"Economic signals, farmers' response and environmental change", in *Journal of Rural Studies*, No. 5(2), pp. 149-160.

BUDIANSKY, S. (1995),
Nature's Keepers: The New Science of Nature Management, Weidenfeld and Nicholson, London.

DOYLE, C., ASHWORTH, S. and McCRACKEN, D. (1997),
"Agricultural trade liberalisation and its environmental effects", report to the Land Use Policy Group of the GB Countryside Agencies, Scottish Agricultural College, Edinburgh.

DWYER, J. and HODGE, I. (1996),
Countryside in Trust: Land Management by Conservation, Amenity and Recreation Organisations, Chichester, John Wiley and Sons.

ENDICOTT, E. (ed.) (1993),
Land Conservation Through Public/Private Partnerships, Washington, DC, Island Press.

FEATHER, P, HELLERSTEIN, D. and HANSEN, L. (1999),
"Economic Valuation of environmental benefits and the targeting of conservation programs: The case of the CRP", Agricultural Economic Report No. 778, Resource Economics Division, Economics Research Service, US Department of Agriculture, Washington, DC.

HANLEY, N., KIRKPATRICK, H., SIMPSON, I., and OGLETHORPE, D. (1998),
"Provision of public goods from agriculture", in *Land Economics*, No. 74(1), pp. 102-113.

HANLEY, N., WHITBY, M. and SIMPSON, I. (1999),
"Assessing The Success of Agri-Environmental Policy in the UK", in *Land Use Policy*, No. 16(2), pp. 67-80.

HODGE, I.D. (1989),
"Compensation for Nature Conservation", in *Environment and Planning* A, No. 27(7), pp. 1027-36.

HODGE, Ian (1994),
"Rural Amenity: Definition, Property Rights and Policy Mechanisms", Chapter 2, pp. 23-40, in Organisation for Economic Co-operation and Development, *The Contribution of Amenities to Rural Development*, Paris, OECD.

HODGE, Ian (2000),
Agri-environmental relationships and the choice of policy mechanism. *The World Economy* 23 (2) 257-273.

HODGE, I. CASTLE, R. and DWYER, J. (1993),
"Covenants for Conservation: Widening the Options for the Control of Land", in *Ecos*, No. 13(3), pp. 41-45.

HUYLENBROECK, G. and WHITBY, M. (eds.) (1999),
Countryside Stewardship: Farmers, Policies and Markets, Pergamon, Amsterdam.

MENDELSON, R. (1994),
"Property Rights and Tropical Deforestation", in *Oxford Economic Papers*, No. 46 (Supplementary Issue), pp. 750-756.

MERLO, M. (1995),
"Common Property Forest Management in Northern Italy: A Historical and Socio-Economic Profile", in *Unasylva*, No. 46, pp. 58-63.

MERLO, M. (1996),
"Commoditisation of Rural Amenities in Italy", pp. 85-95 in Organisation for Economic Co-operation and Development, *Amenities for Rural Development: Policy Examples*, Paris, OECD.

MERLO, M., MILOCCO, E., PANTING, R, and VIRGILIETTI, P. (2000),
"Transformation of environmental recreational goods and services provided by forestry into recreational environmental products" in *Forest Policy and Economics* (forthcoming).

OECD (1995),
Niche Markets as a Rural Development Strategy, Organisation for Economic Co-operation and Development, Paris.

OECD (1999),
Cultivating Rural Amenities: An Economic Development perspective, Organisation for Economic Co-operation and Development, Paris.

POTTER, C., LOBLEY, M. and BULL, R. (1999),
"Agricultural liberalisation and its environmental effects", Report to the Land Use Policy Group of the GB Countryside Agencies, Wye College, University of London.

RUSSELL, N. (1993),
"Efficiency of rural conservation and supply control policies, *European Review of Agricultural Economics*, No. 20(3), pp. 315-326.

SCHEELE, M. (1999),
"Environmental services provided by agriculture: The setting of environmental targets and reference levels", Paper presented at the workshop on Non-Trade Concerns in a Multifunctional Agriculture, Gran, Norway.

TRAILL, B. (1988),

"The rural environment: what role for Europe?", pp. 78-86 in Whitby, M. and Ollerenshaw, J. (eds.): *Land Use and the European Environment*, Belhaven Press, London.

WIEBE, K. and MEINZEN-DICK, R. (1998),

"Property rights as policy tools for sustainable development", in *Land Use Policy*, No. 15(3), pp. 203-215.

ZILBERMAN, D., KHANNA, M. and LIPPER, L. (1997),

"Economics of new technologies for sustainable agriculture", in *The Australian Journal of Agricultural and Resource Economics*, No. 41(1), pp. 63-80.

Comments by Mary Bohman, Economic Research Service, USDA

Hodge's paper clearly illustrates several innovative programs to provide rural amenities using a combination of private and public sector initiatives. Similar creativity has led to rural land preservation in the United States (Wiebe *et al.*). My comments focus on putting Hodge's conceptual framework in a broader context. In this setting, principles for policy design emerge.

Farmers produce food by choosing a technology and using their own labour, land, capital, and other purchased inputs. Positive and negative externalities and public goods can be associated with each of the inputs and the agricultural product. Examples include pollution from fertiliser, cultural heritage linked to choice of an historic technology, as well as scenic vistas from dairy farms. Figure 7 shows a schematic with the linkages between inputs and outputs and expands on Hodge's two-dimensional chart that relates countryside services to agricultural output. Note that while there are only three ovals on the chart, externalities can be associated with output and each of the inputs. The key message is that a complex and dynamic relationship exists between inputs, outputs, and externalities.

Figure 7. **Physical relationship between agricultural inputs, outputs and externalities**

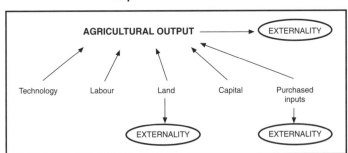

When deciding what to produce and how, farmers consider these physical relationships, but also take prices, risk, and other economic factors into account when making decisions. In making decisions farmers operate like other business people and maximise profits. Economists integrate the physical relationships with market factors and express farmers choice of quantity to maximise profits as a function of the prices of alternative outputs, prices of inputs, and technology and other factors such as risk. As explained by Hodge, externalities are a product of market failures. The price of either the input or output does not include the costs or benefits of the externality and producers may have little incentive to alter activities that contribute to pollution, for example, or to provide rural amenities because these external costs or benefits do not enter their private costs of production. Thus in spite of physical relationships, externalities are not included in the economic decision.

Often, government policies in the form of regulations (such as standards, bans, and restrictions on input use) and incentive based mechanisms (such as taxes, subsidies, and marketable permits) are implemented as corrective mechanisms. Effective policies need to take into account the complex relationships between inputs and outputs, particularly the ability of farmers to change most aspects of farming over time. Hodge's simple relationship between agricultural output and countryside services is misleading because agricultural output can change with little or no impact on countryside services. For example, while dairy production requires cows that produce manure, the pollution from that manure varies as a function of a large number of factors. The location of a farm determines whether nitrogen from the manure can reach groundwater and potentially pollute drinking water. Farmers in environmentally sensitive areas can reduce or eliminate pollution by installing concrete lined pits. Similarly, rural landscapes associated with dairy farms are not directly related to milk output. Farmers can increase milk output through more intensive management that improve production efficiency per cow. The implication for policy is that changes in the output of milk have only an indirect relationship to externalities associated with dairy production.

Given the complex nature of the physical and economic relationship between inputs, outputs, and externalities in agriculture, policies are most effective when they directly affect the specific market failure. In other words the policy should be targeted towards the goal or objective. If providing rural landscapes is the objective then, policies should directly impact land preservation. If animal production is the source of water pollution, then policies should target pollution and not attempt to reduce pollution by decreasing number of animals such as by lowering output prices. Hodge describes several targeted public and private sector initiatives for rural land preservation in Britain.

Price supports or other national, output linked policies are blunt instruments with limited ability to affect specific externalities. For example, attempting to reduce pollution from hog manure by reducing hog prices could actually increase pollution if farmers increase the number of animals per unit of land to save money. Similarly, dairy farms contribution to rural landscapes could diminish with an increase in milk prices if price and other factors led farmers to consolidate farms to increase profitability.

Not only are price supports ineffective instruments to address externalities, but also they create additional costs or distortions both within the country implementing the policy and in other countries. For example, higher dairy prices increase the supply of milk and cause prices to fall. Lower prices are passed onto other countries via world markets. Thus the impacts of policies in one country spillover to other countries. Thus, policies to increase the price of milk to maintain rural landscapes in one country lower prices in other countries, potentially eliminating their scenic vistas. International spillovers are minimised by the types of local initiatives described by Hodge. Bohman *et al.* provide examples of targeted policies for a range of externalities and public goods associated with agriculture.

References

BOHMAN, M., COOPER, J., MULLARKEY, D., NORMILE, M.A., SKULLY, D., VOGEL, S. and YOUNG, C.E. (1999),
The Use and Abuse of Multifunctionality, Economic Research Service, USDA, and *http://www.ERS.USDA.gov/briefing/wto/multifunc1119.pdf*.

WIEBE, K., TEGENE A. and KUHN, B (1996)
Partial Interests in Land: Policy Tools for Resource Use and Conservation, Agricultural Economic Report No. 744, Economic Research Service, USDA.

Chapter 6

Establishing Effective Incentives in Practice:
the Role of Valuation and Influence of Other Factors

by
Ralph Heimlich
Economic Research Service (ERS), United States Department of Agriculture (USDA)

Incentive programs can be an important element in any effort to preserve or promote provision of rural amenities, particularly where agricultural land owners and operators are involved. This paper discusses the rationale for incentive programs and the role of valuation in actually running such programs, provides examples from US programs, and pursues two case studies of their evolution in the Conservation Reserve Program, and US wetland policy. The paper concludes with summary observations about valuation and the implementation of incentive programs in practice.

I. The nature of public goods

Rural amenities generally meet the two tests for public goods (Hanley, Shogren and White, 1997, p. 42). They are non-rival, because at least some of the benefits they provide are available to all, and one person's consumption does not reduce another person's consumption (Samuelson, 1954). The marginal social cost of providing such a good is zero, implying that the Pareto efficient price is zero. This means that no private firm can profit by providing the public good. This creates conditions for "free riders" who enjoy the good but do not pay for it, which adds to the market failure (Olson, 1965).

In practice, providing any of the rural amenities currently being discussed involves control over the use of land. All "rural amenities" flow from controlling land use at either the extensive margin of production (What land is used for farming?), or at the intensive margin (How is the land used?).

The public good nature of rural amenities motivates collective action and creates a role for government as an intermediary to ensure that sufficient amounts of   129 the desired public good are provided. However imperfectly, government senses social demands for public goods and acts to make a market in which government is the sole buyer by providing incentives to public goods providers that enable them to turn a "profit". For those inclined to mathematical proof, Hanley *et al.* (1997) show that the efficient level of public good provided occurs when the aggregate marginal benefit equals its marginal cost.

Rural amenities flowing from the use of land tend to arise from both positive and negative externalities associated with the primary use of land as an input to agricultural and silvicultural production. The treatment of these externalities depends heavily on property rights institutions in the society in which they occur. A rural amenity can be produced through the elimination of a negative externality, such as reducing nonpoint source water pollution from discharging livestock wastes into streams. In many societies, providing this rural amenity would be considered an obligation of the landowner or producer, because the bundle of property rights is not deemed to include impositions on common resources. In other views, this activity could be limited as a nuisance, but is not associated with public goods. Providing a positive externality, such as maintaining a wetland or providing a bucolic viewshed, is an alternative way of providing rural amenities that is less often viewed as an obligation of land ownership. In what follows, I assume that property rights are considered sufficiently strong that policies *requiring* landowners to reduce negative externalities or increase positive externalities are not politically feasible. Voluntary incentive approaches become the *de facto* recourse. In general, this accurately describes the situation in the US with regard to agricultural land use.

2. Some roles for valuation in policy articulation

Given that government decides to act as a collective buyer for society in the provision of public goods, it has several choices to make. Because budgets are usually limited, government can choose what land to make offers on (or which bids to accept from landowners) to purchase rural amenities. This is the *targeting decision*. Budget constraints are also served by as accurate a valuation of the rural amenities associated with specific parcels as possible. Depending on the policy objectives being pursued, government can balance its willingness to pay for the amenity bundle of characteristics associated with control of the land against the willingness to pay of competitors in land markets who value land as a production input. Because government is a virtual monopsonist for public good attributes of land, it need pay no more than the productive value of land where the amenity value is greater than the productive value. However, because there are many bidders for land with higher productive values, either in agricultural or developed uses, it will not bid on or accept such land unless the amenity value exceeds the productive value. Finally, government can decide what payment instrument to use.

Economists can provide useful information for government at several points in the articulation of rural amenities policies. Direct forms of both market and nonmarket valuation are more or less applicable at these different points. Ex *ante* evaluation can be usefully performed during policy development to give policy makers and the public an idea of the magnitudes of public goods that will accrue relative to their costs. Sometimes the flows of benefits and costs from different approaches to a program can be evaluated, helping policy makers choose between alternatives. Often, however, these studies are based on benefits transfer techniques that extrapolate from relatively few small-area studies to a wider universe of landscapes without having much ability to account for differences in value that arise from the varying quality of the amenity provided. Ex *ante* evaluation is often hampered by incomplete information on how the program will actually be run, and inability to accurately simulate what land will be sought, or how landowners will respond to the incentives offered.

Different kinds of market and nonmarket valuation are appropriate in actually implementing a rural amenities program. Economic theory shows that, in concept, the targeting decision should be guided by comparing the marginal cost and marginal benefit of each parcel, and should focus on those parcels with the highest ratio of benefits to costs, until the budget is exhausted. This course of action is more often impractical than not. Indicators of value that are believed to proxy for the values that cannot be estimated are often used in practice to evaluate the cost-effectiveness of specific choices in implementing rural amenities programs.

The ability to make market and nonmarket valuations of land limits program design choices government can make. Market valuation in the agricultural land market is conceptually quite easy. Landowners' reservation prices for control of land use in agricultural land markets are easily determined using commodity market prices and estimates of production costs. These values are often less than the likely value from controlling use of that land to provide public goods benefits, even though that value cannot be precisely estimated. Where land values are heavily influenced by development expectations, market valuation becomes much more difficult, and there are likely fewer parcels for which the value of public goods provided by maintaining land in rural use exceeds the market values. Beyond keeping the cost of rural amenities programs low, government may choose to meet other policy objectives, such as increasing farm incomes, by choosing to pay based on the value of the land's contribution to public goods. However, paying farmers for the value of the public good produced by keeping the land in a specific use, or operating the land in a specific way, depends critically on being able to estimate nonmarket public goods values for specific parcels quickly and at low cost.

The choice of payment instrument involves other valuation issues. In addition to direct rent, easement, or fee simple purchase, government can use tax expenditures to recompense landowners, or it can leverage existing payments, in effect renegotiating "deals" struck in the past. Rents in agricultural land markets are conceptually

131|

easy to estimate, either through direct observation or by estimating net returns in production. Easement values are complicated by the value of uses or practices not restricted by the easement, such as timber sales or sale or rental of hunting or fishing rights. Fee simple purchase always involves some element of development expectation, which is more difficult to value than agricultural production, but this is relatively minor in rural areas. Tax expenditure, in the form of use value assessment, is a matter of estimating the proportion of value covered by agricultural production relative to development value. In practice, this has been hampered by all the problems of estimating development value, and some political difficulties implied by rising or falling agricultural prices, as well. Another form of tax expenditure used by the US federal government involves deductions from the income tax for donation of a conservation easement under the Internal Revenue Code. This suffers from all the problems of estimating easement values, as well as the technical and often contradictory rulings of the IRS. Finally, using the leverage of existing payments, such as the conservation compliance (sodbuster and swampbuster) provisions of US farm policy, hinges on the ability to estimate the value of those payments to the farmer, which has fluctuated with market conditions and the terms of the programs.

Finally, *ex post* evaluations of rural amenities programs depend on market and nonmarket valuation techniques to estimate whether programs actually implemented achieved successful results. These analyses may inform decisions to continue existing programs, or may be the basis for reformulating or refining programs to more effectively or efficiently provide rural amenities. Ex *post* evaluation is often literally an after thought, or is prompted by problems brought to light only when the program is implemented. In these cases, data on specific characteristics of the parcels affected by the program, either before or after the program was implemented, have often not been collected. Other factors that influence the values, particularly market values, almost certainly have had an influence that must be controlled for, but which may be difficult to determine.

3. US incentive programs for promoting rural amenities from agriculture

Since at least the 1930s, the United States has had a variety of voluntary incentive programs related to the use and management of rural land. While the focus of many of the practices installed under these early programs was on the farm, they were motivated at least in part by dramatic floods, siltation, and dust storms that stemmed from deforestation and poor land management on farms.

3.1. Cost-share programs

Some of the first voluntary programs offered to share the cost of installing soil and water conservation practices. In these early days, cost-share was a viable concept because the transaction was viewed as a joint investment between the landowner, who protected or enhanced his capital investment in land as a productive asset, and the public, who derived benefits from reduced flooding, siltation, and wind blown dust. Born in the Great Depression, these programs also had a strong social purpose in providing income assistance to farmers who might otherwise abandon family farms and migrate to cities, further contributing to an already large public assistance burden. In this context, cost sharing contributed to farm incomes because the labour and machine inputs required to install the practices were self-supplied by the farm operator, with technical assistance from the government.

Among the first cost-share programs were technical assistance, offered under the Conservation Technical Assistance (CTA) program, and financial assistance, offered under the Agricultural Conservation Program (ACP), both authorised in 1936 (Magleby *et al.*, 1995, Figure 3). The Great Plains Conservation Program (GPCP), authorised in 1957, offered an integrated program of technical and financial assistance on entire operating units to producers in the Great Plains states. The Small Watershed Program (PL-566), initiated in 1954, and the Resource Conservation and Development Program, authorised in 1962, were similar programs focused on watersheds or areas, rather than individual farms. By the mid-1970's cost-share programs explicitly for off-site concerns with water quality and other environmental problems emerged in the Colorado River Basin Salinity Control Program, initiated in 1974, and the Rural Clean Water Program (RCWP), begun in 1980. All cost-sharing programs were consolidated in the Environmental Quality Incentives Program (EQIP) in 1996, which has been funded at about $150 million per year. The historical pattern of expenditures on these programs is shown in Table 7. Much of the cost-sharing expenditure in 1936-40 was actually for idling land. Recent cost-sharing expenditures are detailed in Table 8. Recently, the Administration proposed spending $325 million annually on EQIP.

Cost-share programs have evolved away from relatively straight-forward transactions on specific conservation practices towards assistance for more nebulous changes to cropping systems that involve changes to management and approach. For example, nearly 1.5 million acres per year were cost-shared to establish permanent vegetative cover in ACP between 1936 and 1985, while only 510 000 acres annually were cost-shared from 1986-95 (USDA-FSA, 1992 and 1997). Cost sharing for 644 000 acres of integrated crop management and agricultural pollution reduction source reduction systems per year was made in 1991-95. Costs for many of the newer approaches are difficult to identify. Some systems, such as conservation tillage, are actually expected to be more profitable than existing practices, so that the "cost" share is actually more of an incentive payment to motivate adoption. Cost-sharing for conservation tillage, reduced tillage, and no-till was paid on an average of 926 000 acres from 1986 to 1995. Over time, the focus has shifted from practices in which the farm operator has some self-interest motivated by expected

133|

Table 7. USDA conservation expenditures, by activity and program, fiscal years 1983-2000

$ million nominal

Activity/program	1984	1986	1988	1990	1991	1992	1993	1994	1995	1996	1997	1998	1999	2000
1. Technical assistance, extension, and administration:														
Natural Resources Conservation Service (NRCS) programs														
Conservation Technical Assistance (CTA)	293.7	286.7	366.4	396.7	426.5	477.9	515.2	523.2	500.0	538.9	529.2	541.8	547.9	584.8
Great Plains Conservation Program (GPCP)	9.1	8.9	8.7	8.0	8.3	9.1	8.9	9.3	9.1	0.0	0.0	0.0	0.0	0.0
Resource Conservation and Development (RC and D)	16.3	17.4	18.2	23.1	24.2	26.0	29.9	28.3	30.4	29.0	29.4	34.4	35.0	35.3
Watershed Investigations and Survey (planning)	24.3	22.7	20.7	21.1	22.0	22.8	22.8	24.4	23.5	14.0	14.0	11.2	10.4	11.7
– Small Watershed Program	8.7	8.5	8.7	8.8	9.2	9.5	9.5	10.9	10.5	0.0	0.0	0.0	0.0	0.0
– River basin surveys	15.6	14.2	12.1	12.3	12.8	13.3	13.3	13.5	13.0	0.0	0.0	0.0	0.0	0.0
Watershed Protection/Flood Prevention	75.7	77.8	67.7	63.2	70.3	74.3	80.4	77.9	70.0	81.4	72.8	50.0	47.0	43.4
Colorado River Salinity Control Program	0.0	0.0	1.8	4.4	5.9	5.9	5.5	5.5	3.9	0.3	0.0	0.0	0.0	0.0
Forestry Incentives Program (FIP)	1.3	1.2	1.2	1.2	1.2	1.2	1.2	1.3	0.7	0.0	0.0	0.0	0.0	0.0
Water Bank Program (WBP)	0.0	0.0	0.0	0.5	0.7	1.1	1.1	0.4	0.0	0.0	0.0	0.0	0.0	0.0
Wetland Reserve Program (WRP)	0.0	0.0	0.0	0.0	0.0	0.0	4.9	3.5	8.8	6.0	12.0	17.7	13.2	18.3
Environmental Quality Improvement Program (EQIP)	0.0	0.0	0.0	0.0	0.0	0.0	0.0	0.0	0.0	6.5	20.0	38.0	33.1	57.0
Wildlife Habitat Incentives Program (WHIP)	0.0	0.0	0.0	0.0	0.0	0.0	0.0	0.0	0.0	0.0	0.0	5.0	5.0	2.5
Farmland Protection Program (FPP)	0.0	0.0	0.0	0.0	0.0	0.0	0.0	0.0	0.0	0.6	0.1	0.7	0.0	1.1
Conservation Farm Option (CFO)	0.0	0.0	0.0	0.0	0.0	0.0	0.0	0.0	0.0	0.0	0.0	0.0	0.0	0.0
Subtotal NRCS	420.4	414.7	484.7	518.2	559.2	618.3	670.0	673.8	646.4	676.6	677.5	698.7	691.5	754.0
Farm Service Agency (FSA) programs														
Agricultural Conservation Program (ACP)	11.2	10.5	11.2	11.3	10.6	10.8	11.2	11.7	6.0	4.5	0.0	0.0	0.0	0.0
Conservation Reserve Program (CRP)	0.0	10.8	5.6	16.4	5.7	11.4	8.9	4.7	5.3	7.2	38.8	67.1	20.9	0.0
Emergency Conservation Program (ECP)	0.7	0.2	0.2	0.6	0.5	0.8	1.5	1.0	1.8	2.4	4.8	1.5	2.5	0.0
Rural Clean Water Program (RCWP)	0.3	3.4	(0.0)	0.9	0.8	0.4	0.0	0.0	0.0	0.0	0.0	0.0	0.0	0.0
FSA salaries and expenses, conservation	35.3	37.3	61.4	60.2	73.8	72.6	65.3	67.6	62.8	62.8	62.8	62.8	62.8	62.8
Subtotal FSA	47.4	62.1	78.4	89.4	91.4	96.1	87.0	85.0	75.9	76.9	106.4	131.3	86.3	62.8

Table 7. **USDA conservation expenditures, by activity and program, fiscal years 1983-2000** (cont.)

$ million nominal

Activity/program	1984	1986	1988	1990	1991	1992	1993	1994	1995	1996	1997	1998	1999	2000
Extension Service (ES) conservation activities	16.0	16.3	18.1	23.5	29.4	31.1	31.1	32.2	32.2	31.7	31.7	29.6	29.3	28.2
Forest Service (FS) programs														
Forest Stewardship	6.9	6.7	6.8	15.2	22.6	23.9	23.3	25.8	25.9	23.4	23.4	23.9	28.8	28.8
Economic Action Programs	1.2	0.9	2.0	4.2	10.2	15.2	13.7	15.5	16.0	14.5	17.2	11.5	17.3	16.3
Forest Legacy Program	0.0	0.0	0.0	0.0	0.0	4.9	0.0	6.9	0.0	3.0	2.0	4.0	7.0	50.0
Pacific Northwest Assistance	0.0	0.0	0.0	0.0	0.0	0.0	0.0	16.4	17.1	16.0	16.8	15.0	9.0	7.0
Urban and Community Forestry	1.6	1.9	2.0	2.8	21.1	23.8	24.8	27.0	28.3	25.5	25.5	26.8	30.5	39.5
Forestry Incentives Program (FIP)	0.0	0.0	0.0	0.0	0.0	0.0	0.0	0.0	0.0	1.2	0.6	0.6	0.7	0.0
Subtotal FS	9.7	9.5	10.8	22.1	53.8	67.9	71.7	91.7	87.3	83.6	85.4	81.7	93.4	141.7
Subtotal Tech. asst., ext., and admin	493.5	502.6	592.0	653.4	733.8	813.4	859.7	882.7	841.8	868.8	901.0	941.4	900.5	986.7
2. Cost-sharing for practice installation														
FSA programs														
Agricultural Conservation Program (ACP)	174.5	129.7	186.6	187.8	171.6	179.1	182.8	183.0	94.0	70.5	0.0	0.0	0.0	0.0
Conservation Reserve Program (CRP)	0.0	12.4	284.8	118.1	40.9	39.3	32.0	14.5	3.7	1.2	11.0	96.1	182.9	190.3
Emergency Conservation Program (ECP)	16.4	6.6	5.7	17.9	8.8	10.3	42.0	24.0	21.2	27.6	90.3	27.0	81.6	0.0
Rural Clean Water Program (RCWP)	0.0	10.6	2.1	0.3	0.1	0.0	0.0	0.0	0.0	0.0	0.0	0.0	0.0	0.0
Stewardship Incentive Program (SIP)	0.0	0.0	0.0	0.0	0.0	1.8	7.8	10.9	12.1	0.0	0.0	0.0	0.0	0.0
Subtotal FSA	190.9	159.3	479.2	324.1	221.3	230.5	264.6	232.4	131.0	99.3	101.3	123.1	264.5	190.3
FS Stewardship Incentives Program (SIP)	0.0	0.0	0.0	0.0	19.9	0.8	17.8	17.9	18.3	4.5	4.5	6.5	0.0	5.0
NRCS programs														
Environmental Quality Incentives Program (EQIP)	0.0	0.0	0.0	0.0	0.0	0.0	0.0	0.0	0.0	123.5	180.0	162.0	140.9	243.0
Colorado River Salinity Control Program	0.0	0.0	3.1	6.0	8.9	8.8	8.2	8.2	0.6	2.4	0.0	0.0	0.0	0.0
Forestry Incentives Program (FIP)	11.1	9.8	10.6	10.2	12.4	11.5	11.2	11.5	6.0	5.7	5.7	5.7	15.7	0.0
Great Plains Conservation Program (GPCP)	12.3	11.5	11.8	12.9	16.4	16.2	16.4	16.4	6.1	0.0	0.0	0.0	0.0	0.0
Wetland Reserve Program (WRP)	0.0	0.0	0.0	0.0	0.0	0.0	0.1	7.4	9.9	8.0	14.2	0.0	0.0	0.0
Wildlife Habitat Incentives Program (WHIP)	0.0	0.0	0.0	0.0	0.0	0.0	0.0	0.0	0.0	0.0	0.0	25.0	15.0	7.5
Conservation Farm Option (CFO)	0.0	0.0	0.0	0.0	0.0	0.0	0.0	0.0	0.0	0.0	0.0	0.0	0.0	0.0
Subtotal NRCS	23.4	21.4	25.5	29.1	37.6	36.5	35.8	43.5	22.5	139.6	199.9	192.7	171.6	250.5
Subtotal Cost-sharing	214.3	180.7	504.8	353.2	278.8	267.8	318.2	293.9	171.9	243.4	305.7	322.3	436.1	445.8

Table 7. **USDA conservation expenditures, by activity and program, fiscal years 1983–2000** (*cont.*)

Activity/program	1984	1986	1988	1990	1991	1992	1993	1994	1995	1996	1997	1998	1999	2000
													\$ million nominal	
3. Public works project activities (NRCS)														
Emergency Watershed Protection	22.0	79.7	13.5	94.9	20.0	70.0	73.1	133.2	290.6	59.1	186.7	80.0	0.0	0.0
Flood Prevention (operations)	9.9	19.1	11.3	16.0	12.8	21.4	23.8	22.9	0.0	6.0	6.0	7.5	7.8	4.3
Resource Conservation and Development (RCandD)	9.7	7.7	7.0	4.2	5.7	6.5	2.6	4.6	2.5	0.0	0.0	0.0	0.0	0.0
Small Watershed Program (operations)	87.6	80.8	83.4	81.7	82.6	89.6	101.3	106.9	0.0	34.0	34.0	45.0	44.6	35.7
Subtotal NRCS public works projects	129.1	187.3	115.2	196.8	121.1	187.5	200.8	267.6	293.1	99.1	226.7	132.5	52.4	40.0
4. Rental and easement payments (FSA and NRCS)														
Conservation Reserve Program (CRP)	0.0	0.0	760.1	1 393.7	1 590.1	1 612.5	1 510.0	1 728.8	1 711.7	1 710.0	1 659.7	1 594.9	1 324.8	1 387.6
Water Bank Program (WBP)	8.8	8.4	8.4	12.2	13.1	17.1	17.1	7.4	0.9	0.7	0.0	0.0	0.0	0.0
Wetland Reserve Program (WRP)	0.0	0.0	0.0	0.0	0.0	0.0	4.4	86.9	78.8	58.0	73.0	211.8	118.1	190.8
Farmland Protection Program (FPP)	0.0	0.0	0.0	0.0	0.0	0.0	0.0	0.0	0.0	14.4	1.9	17.3	0.0	26.4
Conservation Farm Option (CFO)	0.0	0.0	0.0	0.0	0.0	0.0	0.0	0.0	0.0	0.0	0.0	0.0	0.0	0.0
Subtotal rental and easement payments	8.8	8.4	768.5	1 406.0	1 603.2	1 629.6	1 531.5	1 823.0	1 791.4	1 783.1	1 734.6	1 823.9	1 442.9	1 604.8
5. Conservation data and research														
Agricultural Research Service	63.7	62.4	60.5	73.6	73.6	73.9	74.3	76.7	75.5	76.0	73.5	74.7	74.5	92.8
Cooperative State Research Service	29.6	31.3	33.1	40.6	50.6	53.9	49.8	48.0	50.1	42.8	60.2	64.4	64.3	65.9
Economic Research Service	7.7	4.0	3.1	4.6	5.5	5.8	6.3	5.0	5.0	5.0	5.0	5.0	5.0	5.0
Forest Service (forest research)	109.4	120.1	135.5	150.9	167.6	180.5	182.7	195.0	193.5	177.9	179.8	187.9	198.1	234.6
National Agricultural Library (water quality)	0.0	0.0	0.0	0.3	0.3	0.3	0.3	0.3	0.3	0.3	0.2	0.2	0.2	0.2
NRCS programs														
– Soil surveys	53.5	54.3	67.7	68.1	69.8	72.6	72.6	73.9	72.6	76.2	76.4	76.4	78.3	80.6
– Plant materials centers	4.0	3.9	4.9	7.2	7.9	8.1	8.1	8.9	8.1	8.9	8.8	8.8	9.0	9.2
– Snow surveys	3.9	3.8	5.4	5.4	5.6	5.7	5.7	5.8	5.6	5.9	5.8	5.8	6.0	6.1
Subtotal NRCS	61.4	62.0	78.0	80.7	83.2	86.3	86.3	88.6	86.3	90.9	91.1	91.1	93.3	95.9
Subtotal conservation data and research	271.8	279.8	310.2	350.7	380.9	400.6	399.7	413.7	410.7	392.9	409.8	423.3	435.5	494.5
6. Conservation compliance and sodbuster (FSA and NRCS)								(expenditures are included in other programs listed above)					
USDA total	1 117.5	1 158.7	2 290.5	2 960.0	3 117.8	3 299.0	3 310.0	3 680.9	3 508.9	3 387.4	3 577.8	3 643.5	3 267.4	3 572.0

Source: Aministration's budget request submitted in February, 1999.

Table 8. **Economic losses associated with wetland losses, 1954-1992**

Economic activity	Studies	Mean	Range	Estimated wetlands affected[1]	Total economic losses
	Number	1992 constant $ per acre		Thousand acres	Millions of 1992 constant $
Direct economic losses					
Commercial fisheries	7	$733	$7-1 390	573.6	$421
Damages to public goods – use values					
General recreation	4	$2 710	$105-$9 859	12 850.0	$34 824
Recreational fishing	7	$6 571	$95-$28 845	12 850.0	$84 442
Waterfowl hunting	8	$1 244	$108-$3 101	12 850.0	$15 981
Damages to public goods—nonuse values					
Nonuser values	6	$121 471	$1 155-$347 548	12 850.0	$1 560 906
Nonuser values alternate estimate	4	$118 per capita	$12-$280 per capita	n.a.	$462 576

Note: Based on coastal wetland losses for commercial fisheries and total net losses of 458 000 acres per year in 1954-74, 290 000 acres per year in 1974-83, and 79 000 acres per year in 1982-92 for public goods losses.

on-farm benefits to practices, which provide public good benefits. The share of ACP expenditures devoted to practices with a primary purpose of erosion control declined from 71 per cent in 1998 to 51 per cent in 1995, while the share for practices whose primary purpose was surface water quality improvement grew from 7 per cent to 27 per cent. (USDA-ERS, 1997, Table 6.1.2).

3.2. Land rights programs

By far the largest US voluntary incentive programs have paid producers to idle cropland and restore the vegetation to conserving uses. Since the Great Depression, an unstated objective of such programs has been to reduce production of agricultural commodities, thereby reducing supplies and increasing prices (Heimlich and Claassen, 1999). Consequently, land retirement programs have generally been instituted during agricultural recessions, as can be seen by the relationship between US land retirement and agricultural prices. The limited term, usually 10-15 years, to which US land retirement programs have aspired is another consequence of this preoccupation with supply control. While permanent easements would have cost little more than the 10-15 years of annual rental payments, they would not have accommodated a return to production when commodity prices rose again in their cycle. The evolution of the oldest and largest land retirement program, the Conservation Reserve Program (CRP) is discussed in a case study in the next section.

More recently, land has been permanently retired from agricultural production using easements that make a permanent change in the bundle of property

137|

rights encompassed by land ownership (Wiebe *et al.*, 1996). Long used to acquire rights of way for roads and utility lines, permanent easements have been used since 1929 to acquire easements over land for migratory bird habitat under the Migratory Bird Conservation Act (16 U.S.C. 715), administered by the US Fish and Wildlife Service. Since its inception, the program has acquired more than 4.5 million acres of land for the 93 million acre National Wildlife Refuge System (US-FWS, 1999).

State and local governments have purchased development rights on farm and other rural land to prevent development since 1977, when Maryland and Massachusetts inaugurated the first such program (Buis *et al.*, 1995). As of February 2000, 19 states had purchase of agricultural easements (PACE) programs which had acquired more than 4 000 easements covering more than 663 000 acres (AFT, 2000). Local programs accounted for another 1 186 easements on an additional 156 000 acres. Funding mechanisms include State appropriations, dedicated tax revenues, such as cigarette or real estate transfer taxes, and bond issues. Criteria for eligibility and prioritisation for purchase are as varied and distinctive as the States involved. Selection often turns on the degree of development pressure, the viability of the land and location for agricultural production, and synergy with other parcels in the program, or with other programs aimed at similar objectives (AFT, 1997).

Purchases of development rights programs have been the domain of state and local governments since their inception. In the 1996 FAIR Act, Congress passed the Farmland Protection Program (FPP) which, for the first time, provides Federal funding to State, local, or tribal entities with existing farmland protection programs to purchase conservation easements or other interests in order to keep agricultural land in farming. The goal of the program, run by NRCS, is to protect 170 000-340 000 acres of farmland. Priority is given to applications for perpetual easements, although a minimum of 30 years is required. In fiscal years 1996-98, USDA signed co-operative agreements with states and local governments obligating $33.4 million for development interests. The Administration has recently proposed $65 million per year in additional funding for FPP.

Despite the preference for the flexibility offered by annual rental payments, the large investment required to restore cropland to wetlands justified the use of permanent easements in the Wetland Reserve Program, authorised in the Food, Agriculture, Conservation, and Trade Act of 1990 (Heimlich *et al.*, 1998). Enrolment is nearly complete on the 975 000 acres of former cropland to be restored to wetlands. WRP is discussed further in the wetlands case study. The Administration has recently proposed replacing the overall enrolment cap with an annual goal of 250 000 acres per year.

3.3. Tax programs

Policy makers are fond of providing incentives for voluntary programs through the tax system, possibly because of a kind of "money illusion" associated with tax expenditures. Two examples from the US experience are use value assessment of agricultural and rural land under state property tax law, and deductions for charitable easement donation under the Federal income tax law.

A factor hypothesised as contributing to development of farmland near cities is the disparity between the value of the land, which increasingly reflects the expectation of development, and the stream of earnings available in agricultural production. When land is assessed at development prices for property tax purposes, a very real cost burden is imposed on the operator, which reduces farm profits and is thought to contribute to decisions to abandon farming. Relief from property taxes was first enacted in Iowa in 1939, and Maryland was the first State to enact use value assessment in 1956 (Tremblay *et al.*, 1987). By 1989, all 50 States had enacted some form of use value assessment (Aiken, 1989). While details of each state program differ widely, their success in preserving rural amenities depends on the effective tax reduction and the restrictions imposed against development (AFT, 1997).

Effective tax reduction is partly a function of how use values are calculated – that is, the discounted value of agricultural production relative to current land values (Tremblay *et al.*, 1987, p. 15). How the property tax is administered also plays an important role in real tax reduction because *de facto* assessments at use value and failure to equalise tax effort across jurisdictions can negate the apparent tax reduction (AFT, 1997, p. 158). In rural counties where few other residents or businesses can assume the assessment burden, increased millage rates can offset any gains from reduced assessments. Restrictions on development coupled with use value assessment range from relatively tight contractual agreements, as in California and Minnesota, to relatively weak "rollback" provisions designed to recapture the taxes forgiven (Tremblay *et al.*, 1987, p. 17).

Overall, use value assessment has not been a strong incentive to forego development, and has not been judged as successful in preserving farmland or rural landscapes (AFT, 1997, p. 163; NALS, 1981, p. 63). Based on the $0.73 1995 average tax rate per $100 of assessed full value, US agriculture's $740 billion in land was liable for $5.4 billion in property taxes, while farm real estate taxes paid were $4.9 billion (ERS-USDA, 2000). The $497 million difference is a conservative estimate of the tax expenditure represented by use value assessment because much rural land granted use value assessment is probably not represented in the ERS sampling. Nevertheless, an expenditure of nearly half a billion dollars represents one of the largest programs intended to provide rural amenities.

Politicians have used another aspect of the US tax system, the Federal income tax, to promote certain behaviours related to land ownership deemed to be of social value. Easements are an old and well respected legal means of separating certain rights in land. Congress significantly encouraged private donation of easements on land for conservation purposes in 1964, and later enacted Section 170(*h*) of the Internal Revenue Code in the Tax Treatment Extension Act of 1980, although some categories of particular interest to agriculture were not clarified until 1986 (Hambrick, 1981; Federal Register, 1986). When a landowner grants a conservation easement to a qualified organisation at less than fair market value, the difference between the compensation paid and the fair market value can be deducted as a charitable donation. "Conservation purposes" include land for outdoor recreation, for fish, wildlife, or plant habitat, for open space, including farm and forestland, and for preservation of historically important land or structures. "Qualified organisations" include units of government and certain tax-exempt entities such as land trusts. This tax treatment of conservation easements has become an important tool in estate planning and is the most important economic factor in the growth of land trusts in the US. It has been used for farmland and habitat preservation, and has been contemplated for use in erosion control and water quality protection (Ward *et al.*, 1989).

Issues of valuation loom particularly large in the process and oversight of Section 170(*h*). Not only is the current appreciated value of a particular parcel a relevant consideration, but differences in the tax status and basis of the different landowners also make a huge difference in how successful a bid for donation of an easement becomes. An individual with little or no taxable income (like many farmers) or who has recently acquired the land (thus having a large tax basis in it) will not find such a donation financially attractive. A similar parcel held by an individual with high taxable income in need of sheltering who has held the parcel long enough to accrue significant appreciation can realise significant income tax and estate and gift tax savings that can be carried over several years (Ward *et al.*, 1989). Lawyers specialising in estate and the environment have become skilled in the law and economics of such transactions and in brokering such deals for non-profit organisations. Often, such organisations as The Nature Conservancy play key roles in Federal and state agency acquisition of significant parcels because they can set up deals and pass on the partial interests to government partners when funding becomes available.

3.4. *Conservation compliance*

One class of US programs is viewed as quasi-regulatory, despite the technically voluntary nature of the disincentives offered. Conservation compliance provisions covering highly erodible land and wetlands were first introduced in the 1985 Food Security Act (Reichelderfer, 1985; USDA-ERS 1997, Chapter 6.4). Producers cannot receive farm commodity program payments if they farm highly erodible land without a conservation plan that reduces erosion to acceptable levels, convert highly erodible land to crop production without such a plan (sodbuster), or convert wetlands to crop production (swampbuster). Participation in commodity programs is voluntary: Producers who do not wish to comply can simply opt out of the programs. However, because the economic survival of many farms depended on commodity program payments in the mid-1980s when these provisions were enacted, producers felt that conservation compliance was not voluntary at all.

Over the course of the first decade in which compliance provisions were in force, only about 3 500 producers were found to be in violation of highly erodible land provisions, and about 1 000 in violation of wetland provisions, with a total of about $23 million in commodity benefits denied (USDA-ERS, 1997, Tables 6.4.2 and 6.5.5). Compliance is recognised as at least partly responsible for increasing conservation tillage from about 25 per cent of cropland in 1989 to about 36 per cent in 1996 (USDA-ERS, 1997, Table 4.2.1). Compliance, along with agricultural recession in the latter half of the 1980's and early 1990's, is also partly responsible for reducing conversion of highly erodible land and wetlands to crop production (Heimlich *et al.*, 1998; Heimlich and Melanson, 1995).

4. Evolution of incentive program design: CRP and Wetlands case studies

In this section, two case studies of US experience with voluntary incentive programs at the Federal government level are presented: the Conservation Reserve Program and wetland programs. The emphasis is on how the programs were actually implemented, their evolution over time as experience was gained in operating them, and the roles valuation played and did not play in their implementation.

4.1. *Case Study: Conservation Reserve Program*

The first US agricultural land retirement program began in the Depression of the 1930s. The Cropland Adjustment Act of 1934 retired about 20 million acres in the two years of its existence (Crosswhite and Sandretto, 1991). Most land retirement in the 1930's was actually accomplished under cost-share programs rather than explicit CRP-like programs (Kramer and Batie, 1985). The original Conservation Reserve Program was established under the Soil Bank Act (70 Stat. 188; 7 USC 1801-1837) in 1956 as agricultural prices declined following World War II. Landowners received cost-share payments to establish conservation cover and annual rental payments for 3 to 10 years. At its peak in 1960, 306 186 farms enrolled 28.7 million acres. The last land in this program came out of contract in 1972 (ASCS, 1970; Aines, 1963).

Under the Soil Bank, CRP was generally regarded as a very successful program. It reduced acreage and stabilised production after the World War II expansion, put money in the pockets of farmers at a time when commodity prices were falling, stabilised fragile soils in the Midwest and Great Plains states during a time of drought when conditions resembling the Dust Bowl could have emerged again, and provided observable changes in habitat and populations of pheasants and other wildlife (Berner, 1989, Edwards, 1983). Little or no evaluation of these programs was ever conducted, especially any studies to comprehensively estimate monetary benefits from the costs incurred in retiring land and establishing cover. There was an analysis of the reuse of land released from CRP contracts, and a limited formal evaluation of a much less extensive pilot program, the Cropland Conversion Program, which operated in 1963-1967 (Aines, 1963; Vermeer, 1967; Kurtz *et al.*, 1980). Most of this evaluation concerned itself with slippage in providing supply control, the cost of reducing output, and the extent to which cover was retained after contracts expired.

The modern Conservation Reserve Program was enacted in the 1985 Food Security Act (FSA) and authorised initially at 45 million acres. At the brink of agricultural recession, there was little need for *ex post* analysis of the previous CRP, nor *ex ante* analysis of the proposed program to convince Congress that retiring cropland could help improve the agricultural economy and contribute to soil, water, and wildlife habitat objectives. Analysis that was undertaken by economists focused largely on the how the supply control mechanism would work, and how auctions could promote efficiency in running such a program (Boggess and Heady, 1981; Dicks, 1985; Ervin and Mill, 1985).

Most of these considerations were not relevant as the program was actually implemented. The 45 million acre goal effectively precluded auctions because it was impossible to enrol that much acreage in a short period. Multiple enrolment periods and the obvious pressure government officials were under to enrol as much land as quickly as possible opened opportunities to game any bidding system in favour of the landowner. The sheer volume of offers overwhelmed local officials ability to judge even appropriate rental rates, let alone the relative benefits offered by respective parcels. Some 65 000 contracts for 8 million acres were accepted in 3 signups in 1986 (Osborn *et al.*, 1995). What began as an auction experiment quickly became an offer system as landowners tested the program's limits and maximum acceptable rental rates (MARR) were established. Even if benefits could somehow have been estimated that accurately reflected relative differences between so many parcels, the overwhelming mandate to enrol acres would have negated any cost/benefit or cost/effectiveness enrolment criteria.

In terms of the earlier discussion in the first section of this paper, by accepting offers based on prevailing cash rents, government chose to deal in the agricultural land market, rather than a market for rural amenities. It also implicitly chose to exclude land in urbanising areas because the MARRs were based on agricultural rents, rather than rentals implied by values in developed use. Finally, the MARRs were a tacit admission that government officials implementing the program in local offices were unable to apply even the rudiments of market valuation for agricultural land, which are well understood and practised in appraisal technique for specific parcels, let alone attempting nonmarket valuation of rural amenity attributes. Beyond lack of valuation training, the principal practical obstacle to developing systematic appraisals of the offered parcels was the volume of parcels offered and the short time frame for enrolment decision making.

Only one innovation over the original CRP of the 1950's was adopted for the new CRP: enrolment was targeted to highly erodible land (Heimlich and Bills, 1984). The highly erodible land criteria were originally developed to implement the conservation compliance and sodbuster provisions that attempted to rationalise incentives created for cropping highly erodible land with erosion control objectives (Reichelderfer, 1985). Conservation compliance and CRP were seen as being coupled: CRP offered an economically feasible way for a farmer with highly erodible land requiring expensive conservation practices to meet compliance requirements. This provision implicitly recognised that soil erosion reduction was the primary environmental objective of the program and focused CRP on the land with the greatest inherent capacity to produce erosion. As implemented, however, the highly erodible criteria were so diluted that nearly 101 million acres were eligible to bid (Osborn et al., 1995). With minor exceptions, every eligible acre bid at a rent under the MARR was accepted.

Criticism of various aspects of this program surfaced in the late 1980s, several touching on valuation issues (GAO, 989; Richelderfer and Boggess, 988). The primary criticism derived from single-minded pursuit of the acreage goal: the "best" acres were not being sought because every eligible acre was accepted. However, even the critics had a rather narrow focus on soil erosion, ignoring other environmental problems that could be addressed with the program. Another criticism was that the MARRs, set for multiple county areas, were often much higher than average county rents resulting in a higher cost for the program than necessary (GAO, 1989). Even where the MARR approximated average rents, a single payment rate created windfalls for landowners with less valuable land and discouraged landowners with more valuable land from participating. Despite these criticisms, a cost/benefit analysis of the program conducted using benefits transfer methods after 26 million acres had been enrolled estimated that the full CRP would produce a net benefit of $3.4 to 11 billion (Young and Osborn, 1990). Income gains to landowners were expected to be more than $13-25 billion, while benefits to natural resources and the environment were valued at only $6-14 billion. Consumer costs were estimated to rise $13-25 billion, due to increased food prices related to reduced production.

Reforms after 1990 FACT Act

The estimated benefits, and continuing problems with the agricultural economy, influenced Congress to extend the program. However, as a result of these criticisms, and because conditions were improving in the agricultural economy, Congress called for changes in the way CRP was administered. In the 1990 Food, Agriculture, Conservation and Trade (FACT) Act, the acreage cap was reduced from 45 million to 36 million acres, reducing pressure to enrol all eligible acreage and creating conditions for more truly competitive signups for the 5 million acres remaining under the cap. Congress also reiterated their 1988 appropriations act direction that CRP rental rates reflect prevailing local rental rates for comparable land. Finally, Congress emphasised a more complete range of environmental goals beyond reducing soil erosion.

In response to this congressional direction, USDA completely revised the CRP bid acceptance process in 1991 (Barbarika *et al.*, 1994). First, the MARRs were replaced by soil-specific rental rates that adjusted the observed county average cash rent up or down based on an index of relative soil productivity. Landowners could bid less than this rate, but the soil-specific rental rate offered to prospective bidders more closely matched the true value of the land being offered. Second, an environmental benefits index (EBI) designed to proxy for the range of environmental benefits being sought by enrolling the land was evaluated for every parcel of land offered. The EBI included terms for:

- improvements in surface water quality;
- improvements in groundwater quality;
- maintenance of soil productivity;
- assistance to producers with potential problems implementing conservation compliance plans;
- acreage planted to trees;
- acreage within identified critical water quality problem areas;
- acreage within conservation priority areas designated by Congress.

A national cost-effective ranking based on the EBI score and offered rental rate was constructed for each signup. Bids with the highest ratios were accepted until the acreage enrolment objectives for the signup were met.

An important aspect of any such system of indicators intended to proxy for the rural amenity values produced is the relative weight given to each component (*e.g.*, Is water quality twice as important as tree planting? Or half as important?). While traditional textbooks on policy analysis leave such choices to the policy-maker, in the case of CRP's EBI, policymakers refused to explicitly judge the relative weights appropriate to each part of the index, deferring to a committee of technical experts which had devised the index components. They, in turn, were unable to agree on anything other than an equal weighting for each component. In practice, policymakers insisted on estimates of where future CRP enrolments using the new processes were likely to occur and seemed satisfied with the geographic shifts from the Great Plains to the Corn Belt and Northeast that were expected with the new system. If equal weighting had not produced a satisfactory geographic shift, it seems likely that some adjustment of factor weightings would have been required until expected enrolment conformed to policymakers' prior assumptions.

The cost-effective criteria adopted for the CRP bid assessment do not provide an objective cost/benefit measure to endogenously judge the program's accomplishments. However, differences between results achieved in the first 9 signups before 1990 and the post-1990 signups indicated improvement in the following ways:

- only 27 per cent of post-1990 enrolment was located in the Great Plains, whereas as 59 per cent of pre-1990 enrolment was located there;
- post-1990 rents averaged $60 per acre, compared with $49 per acre in previous signups;
- 12 per cent of post-1990 enrolment was for tree planting, compared to 6 per cent in previous signups;
- post-1990 erosion reduction averaged 16 tons per acre, compared with 14 tons per acre in the last pre-1990 signup;
- two-thirds of erosion reductions after 1990 were water-caused erosion, while previous erosion reduction was dominated by wind-caused erosion;
- 15 per cent of post-1990 enrolment was in designated conservation priority areas, compared with 2 percent in previous enrolments (Osborn, 1993).

These results indicated that the post-1990 bid acceptance processes were targeting more expensive land in the Corn Belt and Northeast, with higher sheet and rill erosion rates, impacting water quality problems. Reforms of CRP bid acceptance processes were developed after all but 5 million of the 36 million acres authorised for CRP had been enrolled. Despite this, these procedures were given a good test prior to reauthorization of the program in the 1996 Federal Agriculture Improvement and Reform (FAIR) Act.

A more formal validation of the new procedures was accomplished in an *ex post* evaluation of signups 1-12 and the new procedures (Feather *et al.*, 1999). They found that EBI criteria increased freshwater-based recreation and wildlife-viewing benefits, and decreased pheasant-hunting benefits compared with CRP acreage accepted prior to 1992. Based on this partial accounting of benefits, the new procedures increased the benefits $370 million. They also summarised valuation literature associated with various components of the existing EBI.

Reforms after 1996 FAIR Act

Reauthorization of CRP in 1996 FAIR appears to contradict the general trend for land retirement in periods of agricultural recession. In the early 1990s, agricultural prices were rising and US agriculture was finally emerging from a trough that bottomed in 1987. Two forces united to ensure that CRP would be reauthorised. First, a broad coalition of environmentalists, farmers, hunters, community leaders, and wildlife managers who had seen benefits from CRP lobbied hard to prevent 36 million acres in established cover from returning to crop production (Wildlife Management Institute, 1994; Diebel *et al.*, 1996; Taff, 1993 and Cook, 1994). There was clear recognition that much of this land had been idled in the programs of the 1930's and 1960's, and that the current program represented a significant ($25 billion) investment in the environment that should not be casually abandoned. Second, a conservative coalition in congressional agricultural committees pushed through fundamental reform of farm income and commodity programs, discarding price support and set aside programs going back 60 years to the Great Depression (Orden *et al.*, 1996). One part of the transition to a more market-based agricultural system was to prevent the supply increases that 36 million acres of cropland returning to production could create (Heimlich and Osborn, 1993; Osborn and Heimlich, 1994).

The new bid acceptance procedures developed after the 1990 FACT Act were judged successful, although adjustments to some terms were deemed necessary. Several iterations were tried in successive signups, eventually resulting in the current version of the EBI (USDA-FSA, 1999). Because land included in designated conservation priority areas (CPAs) did not have to meet highly erodible land or other eligibility criteria, many proposals were put forward for additions to this list. Much of North and South Dakota and western Minnesota was included in the Prairie Pothole CPA, focused on restoring pothole wetlands for duck habitat, and a large crescent of land across the Southeast was included in the longleaf pine CPA, focused on reforestation with a declining native tree species. While these additions added greatly to the pool of eligible land, committing to wetland restoration or longleaf pine replanting is rather expensive and served to limit the number of offers actually accepted in these CPAs.

Another feature added to CRP was the continuous signup for filter strips and other partial-field enrolment. This was part of a compromise with critics of the high cost and limited effectiveness of whole-field land idling in addressing environmental problems associated with agriculture, and partly with agricultural commodity groups who objected to continued land retirement (Hoefner, 1994; Abel, Daft and Early, 1994). They advocated putting more resources into intensive margin programs such as the new Environmental Quality Improvement Program (EQIP) that consolidated all previous USDA cost-sharing programs. The continuous signup provision for filter strips, windbreaks, and other partial-field enrolments met some of these criticisms because it enrolled less land, focused on intercepting sediment, nutrients and pesticides in runoff from upstream fields rather than idling those fields, and was thought to be more acceptable to farmers in urbanising areas of the

Northeast and California that had previously not enrolled in the regular CRP. The continuous signup and a related Federal/State program called the Conservation Reserve Enhancement Program (CREP) eventually became a focus of USDA's contribution to the Administration's Clean Water Action Plan (Clean Water Action Plan, 2000; USDA-NRCS, 1999).

The reauthorised CRP now had to contend with the massive and predictable number of contracts expiring from the original enrolments in CRP under the 1985 FSA, as well as leave some acreage for the continuous signup (USDA-ERS, 1997, Chapter 6.3). With the 13th signup, it became obvious that merely taking the highest ranked acreage offered in each signup would not necessarily lead to enrolling the best acreage over the life of the entire program. Enrolling the lowest ranked acreage in the 13th signup could preclude enrolling higher rated acreage in contracts that did not expire until later signups. To avoid this, a process of simulating acreage "likely to bid" over the life of the program was developed to estimate the 36 million "best" acres likely to be offered over the entire signup history. The EBI cut-off for each signup was then based on the EBI of the marginal acre in this "long run likely to bid" simulation. An acreage allowance was made for the continuous signup and CREP, assumed to have higher environmental benefits and lower costs than whole-field enrolment in the regular signup, which would be enrolled later.

The continuous signup and CREP pose other valuation challenges. When offered, enrolment was less than expected, prompting calls for "bonuses" and other signup incentives. Rationales for these bonuses range from limited (50%) cost-share rates for fencing and other expensive required practices, supposedly higher value for smaller parcels, thin cash rental markets in North-eastern States, and high transaction costs for the relatively small total payment for a few acres. Determining what are appropriate market rates for such partial-field enrolments is difficult because relatively few transactions of this kind occur in the usual agricultural land markets. Although government would like to be just another buyer in a well-defined rental market, the characteristics of this program push it toward being the sole buyer in a very limited market, with few market signals as to the appropriate rent to elicit participation.

Under US regulatory policy, the proposed rule implementing the reauthorised CRP was determined to be Economically Significant and was reviewed by the Office of Management and Budget (OMB) under Executive Order 12866. An initial benefit/cost assessment was prepared, which was admittedly incomplete because it did not attempt to include any measure of the value of the benefits gained from enrolling the environmentally sensitive cropland in CRP, which is the primary purpose of the program (Federal Register, 1996). Subsequent to issuance of the final rule, a more complete benefit/cost and environmental risk assessment was conducted (Federal Register, 1997). It analysed the economic, environmental, and budgetary impacts of three alternative simulated CRP enrolment scenarios. While demurring

147|

any attempt at comprehensive estimation of CRP benefits, the assessment estimated soil productivity benefits ranging from $150-$195 million annually, water quality benefits ranging from $350-$455 million, and increased consumptive and non-consumptive uses of wildlife ranging from $1.5-$2.0, totalling $2.0-$2.7 billion per year for a partial accounting of the environmental benefits.

Enrolment was expected to increase annual net farm income by $5.8-$7.6 billion. The net economic costs, summing the impacts on farm income, increased CRP outlays, and increased expenditures for a smaller quantity of commodities, ranged from $0.9-$1.5 billion per year.

Comparison of the rough approximations of environmental benefits derived from the estimates for currently enrolled acreage, with the economic cost estimates resulted in total estimated annual benefits to society that exceed costs by $1.1-$1.2 billion. However, due to the uncertainty of the magnitude of errors of the environmental benefits estimates, the authors concluded that likely net impacts to society from CRP would be greater than these estimates.

4.2. Case study: Wetlands Policy

Wetlands are another rural land use that provide a wide variety of benefits, but which have public goods characteristics. Most of this case study is drawn from Heimlich et al. (1999) and Heimlich et al. (1998).

It is now commonly accepted that wetlands provide valuable environmental benefits. However, in the United States they have been converted to other uses, destroying and degrading wetland functions and values from the earliest colonial times. Wetlands were considered a hindrance to settlement and land development; a nuisance that needed to be eliminated. As settlement spread across the land, wetlands were converted for other uses, primarily agriculture, with the pace increasing as available nonwetlands decreased and drainage technology improved. By 1992, 45-50 per cent of the original wetlands in the 48 states had been converted to other uses, with losses approaching 90 percent in Illinois, Indiana, Iowa, Missouri and Ohio (Dahl, 1990).

Market failure is a principal underlying cause of wetland conversion in the United States because the interplay of market forces cannot sustain the socially optimal balance between conversion and conservation. The costs of losing wetlands are shifted to society, rather than internalised by the producer. The cost of conversion is artificially lowered because the public functions and values generated by wetlands are not marketable and are not considered in the private landowner's calculation of benefits and costs (OECD, 1996, p. 51). Another underlying cause of conversion in excess of socially desirable levels is that information about wetlands is not complete. Scientific information is less than complete, including knowledge of how wetlands and other components of ecosystems function together. Practical application of wetland science to the problem of delineating wetlands to be protected from other lands is also a problem. Most important, the economic linkages between wetlands functions and services that have values to humans are not well understood.

Losses from Wetland Conversion

Direct economic losses from losses of US wetlands have not been systematically measured. Most well documented are estimates of the marginal value of wetlands for commercial coastal fisheries. The mean value per acre from 7 studies in Florida, Louisiana, Michigan, and Virginia is $733 (in 1992 dollars), with estimates ranging from $7 to $1 390 (Table 3; Farber and Costanza, 1987; Lynne *et al.*, 1981; Fischer *et al.*, 1986; Bell, 1989; Batie and Wilson, 1979; Farber, 1996; Amacher *et al.*, 1989; summarised in Heimlich *et al.*, AER). With losses of marine and estuarine wetlands totalling 370 900 acres in 1954-74, 118 900 acres in 1974-83, and 83 800 acres in 1982-92, these values imply losses of $421 million since 1954.

Economic values associated with nonmarketed goods associated with species dependent on wetlands include values for general recreation, recreational fishing, and hunting. Mean estimated recreation values from 4 studies averaged $2 710 per acre (in 1992 dollars), ranging from $105 to $9 859 (Farber and Costanza, 1987; Farber, 1996; Leitch and Hovde, 1996). Estimated values for fishing in 7 studies averaged $6 571 per acre, ranging from $95 to $28 845 (Amacher *et al.*, 1989; Thidodeau and Ostro, 1981; van Vuuren and Roy, 1993; Bell, 1989 and Farber, 1996). Values for waterfowl hunting from 8 studies averaged $1 244 per acre, ranging from $108 to $3 101 (van Vuuren and Roy, 1993; Thibodeau and Ostro, 1981; Gupta and Foster, 1975 and Farber, 1996). Assuming all wetlands have these values, losses of 12.9 million acres in 1954-92 imply losses of $34.8, $84.4, and $15.9 billion for general recreation, recreational fishing, and waterfowl hunting, respectively, from wetland losses since 1954.

Economic losses from nonuser's willingness to pay (WTP) for existence and option values of wetlands per person are estimated to average $118 per year, ranging from $12 to $280 (Whitehead and Blomquist, 1991; Loomis *et al.*, 1990 and Poor, 1997). The per capita WTP yields an estimate of $462.5 billion for nonuser values. Per acre values estimated from 4 studies have a mean of $121 471 per acre (in 1992 dollars), ranging from $1 155 to $347 548 per wetland acre. Assuming that all wetland losses affect these nonuser values implies an economic loss of $1.6 trillion for wetland losses since 1954, valued per acre of wetlands lost. Large values per acre result from relatively large willingness-to-pay values per individual derived from contingent valuation studies that are then applied to large populations, and probably overestimate these values.

149|

Restricting consideration to direct economic losses and losses of public goods by wetland users reduces total estimated economic losses to $136 billion, or an imputed average of $10 558 per acre of wetlands lost. Adding the alternate estimate of nonuser values brings the total to $598.2 billion, or $46 556 per acre lost since 1954.

Wetland Conservation Incentive Programs

Over the course of the last 25 years, the Federal government of the United States has implemented four major classes of wetland conservation incentive measures. These measures spanned the gamut from direct regulation, through elimination of direct and indirect wetland conversion incentives, to subsidies for wetland conservation (Heimlich *et al.*, 1998). In general, measures adopted in the 1980s and 1990s were implemented in an incremental fashion, on the pragmatic grounds that measures adopted earlier failed to control wetland losses, presented inconsistencies with previous policies, or proved inadequate to support ecosystem function with conservation alone.

While it might be expected to be a last resort after other measures were enacted, direct regulation of wetland conversion was the first measure enacted. Section 404 of the 1972 Federal Water Pollution Control Act Amendments directs US Army Corps of Engineers and the Environmental Protection Agency to regulate discharge of dredged and fill material into "waters of the United States" (PL 92-500). Section 404 was preceded by a few State laws, and spawned more, resulting in some form of wetland regulation in 44 of the 50 States (Kusler *et al.*, 1994).

The second major policy measure was Executive Order 11990, signed by President Carter in 1977. This order directed federal agencies to minimise destruction, loss or degradation of wetlands and to preserve and enhance the natural beneficial values of wetlands in all actions involving federal lands, federally financed or assisted construction projects, and other federal activities affecting land use. The practical impact of the order, as implemented throughout the Executive Branch Departments, was to deny direct subsidies for wetland conversion (USDI, 1988, p. 27).

The third class of incentive policies eliminated important indirect incentives for wetland conversion. Indirect government assistance for wetland conversion, in the form of farm program benefits and income tax deductions, was largely eliminated by the so-called "Swampbuster" provisions of the 1985 Food Security Act and changes in the 1986 Tax Reform Act (PL 99-198 and 99-514; Heimlich and Langner, 1986 and Heimlich, 1994). A condition on continued receipt of payments from a voluntary agriculture subsidy program, Swampbuster provisions deny most farm program benefits to farmers who choose to convert wetlands. Benefits at risk include direct payments (*e.g.*, production flexibility contract payments), price support loans, agricultural disaster payments, conservation payments, loans for farm storage facilities, and certain federally insured or guaranteed loans. Benefits may be denied for all fields and all farms in which the violator has a financial interest. Although not specifically directed at wetland conservation, provisions of the Tax Reform Act (TRA) of 1986 also eliminated preferential tax treatment of conversion costs and preferential capital gains treatment from selling land that had appreciated in value due to drainage.

The fourth class of policies provided positive incentives for wetland conservation. Included here are various programs to pay landowners to conserve or restore wetlands, primarily on agricultural land. Not included are programs for outright purchase of title to wetlands for addition to the National Wildlife Refuge system or National Parks (Stewart, 1996, pp. 55-56).

Programs under the US Fish and Wildlife Service include the Small Wetland Acquisition Program (SWAP), wetland restoration efforts under the Partners for Wildlife Program and co-operative efforts under the North American Waterfowl Management Plan. Agricultural wetland conservation and restoration programs include the Water Bank, the Conservation Reserve Program, the Wetlands Reserve Program and the Emergency Wetlands Reserve Program. In general, all of these programs are voluntary efforts to acquire property rights in wetlands varying from short-term rental agreements for 10 years (Water Bank, CRP), through longer-term or permanent easements (SWAP, WRP, EWRP), to outright acquisition (SWAP). All involve some degree of cost sharing for wetland restoration or enhancement.

In the 1990 FACT Act, Congress created the Wetlands Reserve Program (WRP) to purchase permanent easements on former wetlands that had been converted to crop production and restore them as wetlands (Carey *et al.*, 1990 and ERS-USDA, 1994). Ex *ante* analysis of potential benefits had been helpful in getting the legislation passed but was far too aggregate to be a useful guide in implementing the program (Ervin *et al.*, 1991). Methodological studies demonstrated the potential for inconsistent results using positive and normative methods for *ex ante* analysis of such programs where little prior experience provided a database for analyses (Parks *et al.*, 1995). Beginning in 1992 as a pilot program in 9 states, WRP has been expanded to the entire nation. WRP was supplemented with an Emergency Wetland Reserve Program (EWRP) authorised after the 1993 Midwest floods to buy out flood-damaged croplands converted from wetlands that would be too expensive to protect through levee repairs. WRP is capped at a maximum enrolment of 975 000 acres, with nearly all enrolled as of 2000. In the 1996 FAIR Act, WRP was broadened to include cost-sharing and 30 year term agreements, in addition to permanent easements.

Neither the market value nor EBI approaches developed for CRP proved to be useful in administering WRP. In theory, average farmland prices in a county could be adjusted based on differences in productivity to arrive at an easement price on which negotiations could be based. In reality, the most important factor in determining the productivity of wetlands converted to cropland is not soil type, but the degree of drainage achieved in the conversion. Poorly drained wetlands are not very productive in agriculture, despite the fact that well-drained fields of similar soil are typically very productive. Unlike soil type, there is little reliable secondary data on current drainage available. If a field visit is necessary to determine current drainage, the rest of the information needed for a site specific appraisal can be obtained at low marginal cost. In practice, WRP has been administered based on site-specific appraisals.

Despite a large literature estimating nonmarket values of wetlands (see Appendix I in Heimlich *et al.*, (1998) for a summary), very little is known about what features of particular wetland types are associated with higher and lower values. The range of values in the literature for similar functions is very large, indicating that either there is great heterogeneity in wetlands providing similar services, or there is little robustness to the nonmarket methods used, or both. The relationships between wetland characteristics and the physical functions and ecological services they provide are poorly understood. Even if these relationships were determined, there is little secondary data on wetland characteristics collected. WRP places an additional burden on the analyst because the sites offered are former wetlands that must undergo extensive restoration. It is the prospective functions and values of the restored wetlands that must be assessed.

These gaps in understanding and data proved too difficult to overcome in developing an environmental benefits index similar to the CRP's EBI. An index that could be used to indicate the relative cost-effectiveness of enrolling different parcels offered in WRP proved impossible to create. In practice, the subjective judgement of officials administering WRP at the local level is the basis for choices between former wetlands offered for restoration. Once landowners offer land to WRP and the local official makes an assessment and an on-site appraisal, a process of negotiation ensues that may, or may not, result in eventual enrolment. Little or no *ex post* evaluation of the wetland easements acquired and restorations undertaken has been conducted, to date.

5. Incentive programs in practice: conclusions

Based on the US experience with voluntary incentive programs, there are valuable contributions that economics, in general, and the economics of valuation, in particular, can make in structuring these programs, and improving their efficiency and effectiveness. Valuation can play an important role in *ex ante* policy analysis in helping scope programs and bringing out what is to be gained and what costs and unintended consequences may result. Market economic consequences of carefully specified programs often produce results that run counter to expectations of both proponents and opponents in the debate. Valuation studies have not often played an important role in actually implementing incentive programs because the large number of parcels or bids that need to be evaluated and the short time deadlines under which many programs operate. Ex *post* analyses, while they would undoubtedly provide beneficial insights, have seldom been done because the necessary data have not been collected. Program agencies are understandably defensive about *ex post* analyses because it is difficult to separate failures of program design from failures of program implementation.

Economists are attracted to nonmarket valuation issues because there is more unexplored methodological territory in these relatively new areas and society is newly attuned to the importance of nonmarketed benefits. However, US experience with reform of the CRP bid assessment process shows that program implementation can benefit greatly from renewed attention to improvements in market valuation, particularly improvements in data and analysis of land rental markets and easement valuation. As programs focusing on the intensive margin of production evolve, renewed attention to farmers' direct and opportunity costs of adopting new practices and cropping systems will also become increasingly important.

While theory suggests that cost/benefit is the primary tool for assuring program efficiency, the lack of comprehensive benefit measures in practice generally precludes that as a possibility for program implementation. In the US, practical schemes for assessing the cost-effectiveness of specific program choices in the implementation phase have been recognised as improvements that utilise a basic tool of economics and can actually be accommodated by program officials. Cost-effectiveness analysis can also deal with the often messy multiple objective character of real programs as well. Implementing cost-effectiveness criteria involves expert judgement about appropriate indicators and appropriate weights that require collaboration between disciplines, and between technical and policy participants.

Economists can play a significant role in shaping emerging programs for rural amenities. We have long understood the role of economic incentives in motivating producer behaviour and are more attuned to the potential tradeoffs between private opportunities and public benefits. In the practice of economics, it is important that we make use of the full range of tools and techniques available and carefully match them to the situation at hand and the constraints imposed by large, complex programs.

References

ABEL, Daft and EARLEY (1994),
  "Large Scale", *Land Idling Has Retarded Growth of* US *Agriculture*, prepared for National Grain and Feed Foundation, Alexandria, VA, May, 50 pages plus appendices.

AIKEN, J. David (1989),
  "State Farmland Preferential Assessment Statutes", RB-310, Agricultural Research Division, University of Nebraska, Lincoln, NE.

AINES, R.O. (1963),
  "Release of Land from Conservation Reserve Contracts", AER-34, US Department of Agriculture, Economic Research Service, Washington, DC, 18 pages.

AMACHER, G.S., BRAZEE, R.J., BULKLEY, J.W. and MOLL, R.A. (1989),
  "Application of Wetland Valuation Techniques: Examples from Great Lakes Coastal Wetlands", School of Natural Resources, University of Michigan, Ann Arbor, June.

AMERICAN FARMLAND TRUST (1997),
  Saving American Farmland: What Works, American Farmland Trust, Northampton, MA, 334 pages.

AMERICAN FARMLAND TRUST (2000),
  "Fact Sheet: Status of State PACE Programs", Farmland Information Center, Northampton, MA, March, 4 pages, at *http://www.farmlandinfo.org/fic/tas/tafs-pacestate.pdf*.

ASCS-USDA (1970),
  "Final Report, Conservation Reserve Program, Summary of Accomplishments, 1956-1972", US Department of Agriculture, Agricultural Stabilization and Conservation Service, Washington, DC, 17 pages.

BARBARIKA, A., OSBORN, C.T. and HEIMLICH, R.E. (1994),
  "Using an Environmental Benefits Index in the Conservation Reserve Program," in *Proceedings of the NCT-163 Post Conservation Reserve Program Land Use Conference, Denver*, CO, January 10-11, pp. 118-133.

BATIE, S.S. and WILSON, J.R. (1979),
  "Economic Values Attributable to Virginia's Coastal Wetlands as Inputs in Oyster Production", in *Bulletin* 150, Virginia Polytechnic Institute and State University, Department of Agricultural Economics, Research Division, Blacksburg, VA, 34 pages in Anderson and Rockel (1991).

BELL, F. (1989),
  "Application of Wetland Valuation Theory to Florida Fisheries", SGR-95, Sea Grant Publication, Florida State University, Tallahassee, FL, June, in Anderson and Rockel (1991).

BERNER, A.H. (1989),
"The 1985 Farm Act and Its Implications for Wildlife", in Chandler, W. (ed.): *Conservation Challenges. Audubon Wildlife Report*, 1988/89, Academic Press, Inc., pp. 436-465.

BOGGESS, W.G., and HEADY, E.O. (1981),
"A Sector Analysis of Alternative Income Support and Soil Conservation Policies", in *American Journal of Agricultural Economics*, No. 63(4), pp. 618-28.

BUIST, H., FISCHER, C., MICHOS, J. and TEGENE, A. (1995),
"Purchase of Development Rights and the Economics of Easements", AER-718, ERS-USDA, 20 pages.

CAREY, Marc, HEIMLICH, Ralph and BRAZEE, Richard (1990),
"A Permanent Wetlands Reserve: Analysis of a New Approach to Wetland Protection", in *Agriculture Information Bulletin* 610, US Department of Agriculture, Economic Research Service.

CLEAN WATER ACTION PLAN (2000),
Clean Water Action Plan: Restoring and Protecting America's Waters, at *http://cleanwater.gov/*

COOK, K. (1994),
"So Long, CRP", Environmental Working Group, Washington, DC, 38 pages.

CROSSWHITE, W.M. and SANDRETTO, C.L. (1991),
"Trends in Resource Protection Policies in Agriculture", in *Agricultural Resources, Cropland, Water, and Conservation Situation and Outlook Report*, AR-23, ERS-USDA, Washington, DC, pp. 42-46.

DAHL, T. (1990),
"Wetlands Losses in the United States, 1780's to 1980's", US Department of Interior, US Fish and Wildlife Service, Washington, DC, 21 pages.

DICKS, M.R. (1985),
"Aggregate Economic Impacts of a Conservation Easement Program for the Corn Belt", unpublished dissertation, University of Missouri-Columbia.

DIEBEL, P.L., JANSSEN, L.L. and SMITH, K. (1996),
"Economic and Environmental Implications of Expiring Conservation Reserve Contracts", NC-214, Committee Report, 46 pages.

ECONOMIC RESEARCH SERVICE-USDA (1994),
"Agricultural Resources and Environmental Indicators", AHB-705, Chapter 6.4, *Wetlands Programs*, ERS-USDA, pp. 191-200.

EDWARDS, W.R. (1983),
"Early ACP and Pheasant Boom and Bust: A Historical Perspective with Rationale", Proceedings of *Perdix* III: *Gray Partridge/Ring-Necked Pheasant Workshop*, March 28-30, *Campbellsport*, WI, pp. 71-83.

ERS-USDA (2000),
"Balance sheets (assets, debt, and equity) for the farm sector (1960-98)", *http://www.econ.ag.gov/briefing/farmincome/fbsdmu.htm* and "Land Use, Value, and Management -Q and A's-Q. How much is agricultural land taxed?", *http://www.econ.ag.gov/briefing/landuse/Rvalqa7.htm*.

ERVIN, D.E and MILL, J.W. (1985),
"Agricultural Land Markets and Soil Erosion: Policy Relevance and Conceptual Issues", in *American Journal of Agricultural Economics*, No. 67(5), pp. 938-42.

FARBER, S. and COSTANZA, R. (1987),
"The Economic Value of Wetland Systems", in *Journal of Environmental Management*, No. 24, pp. 41-51, in Anderson and Rockel (1991).

FARBER, S. (1996),
"Welfare Loss of Wetlands Disintegration: A Louisiana Study", in *Contemporary Economic Policy*, No. 14(2), pp. 92-106.

FEATHER, P., HELLERSTEIN, D. and HANSEN, L. (1999),
"Economic Valuation of Environmental Benefits and the Targeting of Conservation Programs: The Case of the CRP", AER-778, Economic Research Service, USDA, 56 pages.

FEDERAL REGISTER (1996),
Conservation Reserve Program (CRP)--Long Term Policy, No. 61(185), pp. 49697-49711 (at *http://www.nhq.nrcs.usda.gov/*OPA/FB96OPA/CRPL*ngTm.htm*).

FEDERAL REGISTER (1997),
Conservation Reserve Program – Long Term Policy; Final Rule, No. 62(33), pp. 7601-7635 (at *http://www.nhq.nrcs.usda.gov/*OPA/FB96OPA/CRP*frul.html*).

FISCHER, A.C., HANEMAN, M., HARTE, J., HORNE, A., ELLIS, G. and VON HIPPEL, D (1986),
"Economic Valuation of Aquatic Ecosystems", Final report to the US EPA, Cooperative Agreement No. 811847, October, in Anderson and Rockel, (1991).

GUPTA, T.R. and FOSTER, J.H. (1975),
"Economic Criteria for Freshwater Wetland Policy in Massachusetts", in *American Journal of Agriculture Economics*, No. 57, pp. 40-45, in Anderson and Rockel (1991).

HEIMLICH, R.E., WIEBE, K.D., CLAASSEN, R., GADSBY, D. and HOUSE, R.M. (1998),
Wetlands and Agriculture: Private Interests and Public Benefits, AER-765, Economic Research Service, USDA. 94 pages.

HEIMLICH, R.E., WIEBE, K.D., CLAASSEN, R. and GADSBY, D. (1999),
"Experiences with Incentive Measures to Promote Conservation of Wetlands", document [ENV/EPOC/GEEI/BIO(97)9], Organisation for Economic Co-operation and Development, Paris, May 5th, 40 pages.

HEIMLICH, R.E. and MELANSON, J. (1995),
"Wetlands Lost, Wetlands Gained", in *National Wetlands Newsletter*, No. 17(3), pp. 1-25, May-June.

HEIMLICH, R.E. and BILLS, N.L. (1984),
"An Improved Soil Erosion Classification for Conservation Policy", in *Journal of Soil and Water Conservation*, No. 39(4), pp. 261-266.

HEIMLICH, R.E. and CLAASSEN, R. (1999),
"Conservation Choices for a New Millennium", in *Choices*, Fourth Quarter, pp. 45-48.

HEIMLICH, R.E. and OSBORN, C.T. (1993),
"After the Conservation Reserve Program: Macroeconomics and Post-Contract Program Design", in *Proceedings of the Great Plains Agricultural Council, Rapid City*, SD, June 2-4, 1993, pp. 113-133.

HEIMLICH, Ralph E. and LANGNER, Linda L. (1986),
"Swampbusting: Wetland Conversion and Farm Programs", in *Agricultural Economic Report*, No. 551, US Department of Agriculture, Economic Research Service, Washington, DC.

HOEFNER, Ferd (1994),
"The CRP's Niche in Agricultural Conservation...continued", in *When Conservation Reserve*

Program Contracts Expire: The Policy Options, Conference proceedings, February 10-11, Arlington, VA, pp. 66-70.

KRAMER, R.A. and BATIE, S.S. (1985),
"The Cross-Compliance Concept in Agricultural Programs: The New Deal to the Present", in *Agricultural History*, No. 59(4), pp. 307-319.

KURTZ, W.B., ALIG, R.J. and MILLS, T.J. (1980),
"Retention and Condition of Agricultural Program Conifer Plantings", in *Journal of Forestry*, No. 78(5), pp. 273-276.

KUSLER, J.A., RAY, C., KLEIN, M. and WEAVER, S. (1994),
"State Wetland Regulation: Status of Programs and Emerging Trends", Association of State Wetland Managers, Bern, NY, 178 pages.

LEITCH, J.A. and HOVDE, B. (1996),
"Empirical valuation of prairie potholes: Five case studies", in *Great Plains Research*, No. 6, pp. 25-39.

LOOMIS, J.B., WEGGE, T., HANNEMANN, M. and KANNINEN, B. (1990),
"The Economic Value of Water to Wildlife and Fisheries in the San Joaquin Valley: Results of a Simulated Voter Referendum", in *Trans. 55th North American Wildlife and Natural Resource Conference*, pp. 259-268.

LYNNE, G.D., CONROY, P. and POCHASTA, F. (1981),
"Economic Valuation of Marsh Areas to Marine Production Processes", in *Journal of Environmental Economics and Management*, No. 8(2), pp. 175-186, in Anderson and Rockel (1991).

MAGLEBY, R., SANDRETTO, C., CROSSWHITE, W. and OSBORN, C.T. (1995),
"Soil Erosion and Conservation in the United States: An Overview", AIB-718, Economic Research Service, US Department of Agriculture, 29 pages.

NATIONAL AGRICULTURAL LANDS STUDY (1981),
The Protection of Farmland: A Reference Guidebook for State and Local Governments, US Government Printing Office, Washington, DC, 284 pages.

ORDEN, D., PAARLBERG, R. and ROE, T. (1996),
"Can Farm Policy be Reformed? Challenge of the Freedom to Farm Act", in *Choices*, First Quarter, pp. 4-7.

OSBORN, C.T. (1993),
"The Conservation Reserve Program: Status, Future and Policy Options", in *Journal of Soil and Water Conservation*, No. 48(4), pp. 271-279.

OSBORN, C.T. and HEIMLICH, R.E. (1994),
"Changes Ahead for the Conservation Program", in *Agricultural Outlook*, AO-209, July, pp. 26-30.

OSBORN, C.T., LLACUNA, F. and LINSENBIGLER, M. (1995),
"The Conservation Reserve Program: Enrolment Statistics for Signup Periods 1-12 and Fiscal Years 1986-93", in *Statistical Bulletin*, No. 925, ERS-USDA, 102 pages.

PARKS, P.J., KRAMER, R.A., and HEIMLICH, R.E. (1995),
"Simulating Cost-Effective Wetlands Reserves: A Comparison of Positive and Normative Approaches", in *Natural Resource Modelling*, No. 9(1), pp. 81-96.

POOR, P.J. (1997),
"The Contingent Valuation of Nebraska's Rainwater Basin Wetlands", selected paper presented at the "American Agricultural Economics Association meetings", Toronto, Canada, July, 36 pages.

REICHELDERFER, K.H. (1985),
"Do USDA Farm Program Participants Contribute to Soil Erosion?", AER-532, US Department of Agriculture, Economic Research Service, Washington, DC, 74 pages.

RICHELDERFER, K.H. and BOGGESS, W.G. (1988),
"Government Decisionmaking and Program Performance: The Case of the Conservation Reserve Program", in *American Journal of Agricultural Economics*, No. 70(1), pp. 1-11.

STEWART, R.E. Jr. (1996),
"Wetlands as Bird Habitat", in Fretwell, Judy D., Williams, John S. and Redman, Phillip J. (eds.): *National Water Summary on Wetland Resources*, USGS Water-Supply Paper 2425, US Geological Survey, USDI, Washington, DC, pp. 49-56.

TAFF, S.J. (1993),
"The CRP in the Upper Midwest: What Should We Do Next?", Minnesota Extension Service, University of Minnesota, St. Paul, MN, 16 pages

THIBODEAU, F.R. and OSTRO, B.D. (1981),
"An Economic Analysis of Wetland Protection", in *Journal of Environmental Management*, No. 12, pp. 19-30, in Anderson and Rockel (1991).

TREMBLAY, R.H., FOSTER, J.H., MACKENZIE, J., DERR, D.A., LESSLEY, B.V., COLE, G.L. and BILLS, N.L. (1987),
Use Value Assessment of Agricultural Land in the Northeast, NE Regional Research Publication, Vermont Agricultural Experiment Station Bulletin 694, University of Vermont, Burlington, VT, 24 pages.

USDA, AGRICULTURAL CONSERVATION AND STABILIZATION SERVICE (1992),
Agricultural Conservation Program, 55-Year Statistical Summary, 1936 through 1990, Washington, DC, 58 pages.

USDA, ECONOMIC RESEARCH SERVICE (1997),
"Agricultural Resources and Environmental Indicators, 1996-97", AHB-712, Washington, DC, 347 pages, at *http://www.econ.ag.gov/epubs/pdf/ah712/*

USDA, FARM SERVICE AGENCY (1997),
Agricultural Conservation Program, 60-Year Statistical Summary, 1936 through 1995, Washington, DC, 57 pages.

USDA, FARM SERVICE AGENCY (1999),
"Conservation Reserve Program Signup 20, Environmental Benefits Index", Fact Sheet, September, 6 pages (at *http://www.fsa.usda.gov/pas/publications/facts/ebiold.pdf*).

USDA, NATURAL RESOURCES CONSERVATION SERVICE (1999),
Buffer Strips: Common Sense Conservation, at *http://www.nhq.nrcs.usda.gov/CCS/Buffers.html*.

US DEPARTMENT OF THE INTERIOR (1988),
The Impact of Federal Programs on Wetlands, Volume 1. The Lower Mississippi Alluvial Plain and the Prairie Pothole Region, a Report to Congress by the Secretary of the Interior, Washington, DC, October, 114 pages.

US FISH AND WILDLIFE SERVICE (1999),
News Release July 27, 1999, Hugh Vickery (202) 208-5634 "Migratory Bird Commission Approves $18.5 million for North American Wetland Conservation *http://www.fws.gov/r9extaff/pr9945.html*.

US GOVERNMENT ACCOUNTING OFFICE (1989),
Conservation Reserve Program Could be Less Costly and More Effective, GAO/RCED-90-13, November, 79 pages.

VAN VUUREN, W. and ROY, P. (1993),
"Private and Social Returns from Wetland Preservation versus Those from Wetland Conversion to Agriculture", in *Ecological Economics*, No. 8(1993), pp. 289-305.

VERMEER, J. (1967),
The 1964-65 Cropland Conversion Program: A Description and Appraisal, AER-111, USDA-ERS, Washington, DC, 39 pages.

WHITEHEAD, J.C. and BLOMQUIST, G.C. (1991),
"Measuring Contingent Values for Wetlands: Effects of Information About Related Environmental Goods", in *Water Resources Research*, No. 27(2), pp. 2523-2531, October.

WIEBE, K.D., TEGENE, A. and KUHN, B. (1996),
Partial Interests in Land: Policy Tools for Resource Use and Conservation, AER-744, USDA-ERS, 59 pages.

WILDLIFE MANAGEMENT INSTITUTE (1994),
America Needs the Conservation Reserve Program: A Wildlife Conservation Legacy, Washington, DC, 15 pages.

YOUNG, C.E. and OSBORN, C.T. (1990),
The Conservation Reserve Program: An Economic Assessment, AER-626, USDA-ERS, Washington, DC, 32 pages.

WARD, J.R., BENFIELD, F.K. and KINSINGER, A.E. (1989),
Reaping the Revenue Code: Why We Need Sensible Tax Reform for Sustainable Agriculture, Natural Resources Defence Council, Washington, DC, 142 pages.

Comments by Urs Gantner, Swiss Office of Agriculture

Mr. Ralph Heimlich's paper is clear; it shows how agricultural measures work and how the USDA improves policy measures. In the following, I will comment on some statements made in the paper:

"policies requiring landowners to reduce negative externalities or increase positive externalities are not politically feasible." (Heimlich, p. 2). Comment: In reality it is a combination of enforcement – for example there are laws concerning water protection and environmental protection – and economic instruments – for example there are voluntary incentive approaches.

"government can choose what land to make offers on to purchase rural amenities." (Heimlich, p. 2). Comment: This is the targeting decision. Good targeting requires that the flows of benefits and costs under different conditions are known. Costs can be calculated (for example governmental outlays, societal costs including transaction costs). However, the benefits are more difficult to evaluate: What is the value of a bird? What is the environmental benefit of an environmental program?

"paying farmers for the value of the public good produced ... depends critically on being able to estimate public goods values for specific parcels quickly and at low costs." (Heimlich, p. 3). Comment: Different approaches were discussed at this workshop, for example the valuation of public goods and the environmental benefits index. An alternative approach is: set specific goals, develop policy measures, introduce them, monitor and evaluate, correct and adapt them.

In 1991, the USDA revised the CRP (Conservation Reserve Program): First, landowners can bid for a program. Second, an environmental benefits index (EBI) as a proxy for the environmental benefits is calculated. A cost-effective ranking based on the EBI score and offering rental rates (bids) is constructed. First, the bids with the highest ratios are accepted. Comment: With this approach, efficiency is part of the system. This is really catchy. One question remains however: What about the transaction costs, especially the administration costs, of this approach?

An alternative to the above mentioned approach might be to decentralise environmental measures. Those who benefit, those who decide and those who pay should be the same persons. Why not devise measures on a more regional level and rely on the interest, responsibility and dedication of local (and visiting) people?

Chapter 7

Rural Amenities and their Valuation: Wider Questions for Policy-Makers

by
David Baldock
Institute for European Environmental Policy

While the term "rural amenities" is not necessarily familiar to the multitude of public officials and other stakeholders concerned with rural policy, it refers to a set of issues of growing importance in most OECD countries. Within national boundaries, the impact of agriculture, forestry and other activities on wider social and environmental objectives is no longer a secondary concern, becoming an important force in shaping new policies in many countries. The precise nature of "amenities" varies greatly, potentially extending to a range of public goods, in some contexts including food security, particularly in developing countries. However, an elastic term of this kind helps to capture an expanding set of concerns, not easily satisfied solely by the operation of the market. A similar picture is reflected at the international level, with relatively new issues such as farm animal welfare emerging as "amenity" concerns in a broad sense. At the international level, the intersection of this new agenda with well-established trade concerns is at the crux of the debate.

1. The context

Part of the reason for the sensitivity of the rural amenities debate lies in the difficulty of governments reaching a shared analysis and in the contested nature of much of the information presented in defence of key arguments. It is clear, for example, that proponents of multifunctional agriculture can provide numerous examples to illustrate the types of amenities that can be generated by the farming community. However, it may be less clear how far these cases typify agriculture in a particular sector or geographical region. In principle, convincing methods for valuing these benefits could remove some of the uncertainties. Equally, for those sceptical of the claims for multifunctional agriculture, valuation may address at least part of

161

their concerns, particularly if it illuminated questions about the extent of joint production and the most efficient way of providing amenities. From this perspective,
the workshop is undoubtedly topical and relevant to the concerns of policy-makers.

Agriculture and agricultural policy are the main focus of many of the papers
presented at the workshop. Given the level of interest in agriculture and rural
development policy, and the backcloth of the WTO, this is perfectly appropriate.
However, it should be emphasised that agriculture, and the farming community
engaged in it, are not the only sources of rural amenities. Other economic activities,
including forestry, some crafts and artisanal fisheries, also generate amenities while
others are effectively "provided" by nature.

It is also necessary to see the current international trade and agricultural policy
debates in a wider context. Many OECD Member countries have adopted the language of sustainable development, echoing Agenda 21 to varying degrees. In the
EU for example, sustainable development is now one of the formal objectives of the
Union, embodied in the Treaty of Amsterdam. A number of countries are attempting to improve the integration of environmental and sectoral policies in an effort to
give substance to the often elusive concept of sustainable development. Even if
the steps towards a new policy agenda have been tentative, there is a palpable
shift away from the paradigms of the 1970s and 1980s. Much of the sustainable
development debate has been dominated by the OECD countries but arguably a
shift is now occurring. Since the failed negotiations in Seattle, there has been a
markedly more vigorous effort by some of the leading OECD states to listen to the
concerns of developing countries and to deepen the North-South dialogue.

Sustainable rural development implies a considered balance between economic, social and environmental objectives. This is possible only if policy makers
are equipped with appropriate information and analytical tools with which to structure and inform choices which are usually political rather than technical. Methods
of valuation which answer real policy questions and create confidence amongst
leading stakeholders as well as officials with technical responsibilities would
appear to have much to offer as the sustainability debate deepens. How far existing
methods meet these criteria is a key issue for the workshop, raising questions of
methodological vigour and coherence, cost, administrative and practical utility,
basic data availability, political legitimacy and other issues addressed in earlier
papers. Policy makers in different fields, countries and settings may not answer
these questions in the same way. In the USA, for example, valuation techniques
appear to have established a greater role in policy making than in the EU.

2. Answering policy questions

Policy questions arise from a range of viewpoints. Relatively few start from a
tabula rasa, an open question about the form and level, if any, of public interven-

tion in a particular sphere. This occurs more often with "emerging" issues, such as GMOs than with established areas, of which agricultural policy, with a tradition of multiple interventions, is a prime example. In the agriculture case entrenched political decisions can greatly narrow the scope of short term policy options while potentially creating a demand for analysis and research feeding longer term options, especially those advocated by interests marginalised by the dominant stakeholders. This can occur at the international as well as the national level.

In considering the future utility and demand for valuation techniques and exercises it is essential to consider potential applications. These include:

- *post hoc* policy evaluation;

- prior project and policy cost-benefit analysis;

- valuation of non-market benefits for the purposes of policy design *e.g.*, setting payment rates for incentive schemes or easement values, determining the scope, focus and distribution of such monetary benefits, weighting objectives where budgets are fixed, revising budgets over time, etc.;

- determining the scale of damage to non-market amenities, relevant to the design and operation of a range of policies, including environmental liability legislation, the level of compensation payments, etc.;

- broader policy monitoring and reporting activities, such as environmental accounting;

- comparative policy evaluation, including international comparisons.

It is worth distinguishing between those policy applications where:

- the outcome on the ground is relatively certain and questions of valuation follow from an agreed set of circumstances (*e.g.*, when pollution damage to a river has caused a verifiable number of fish deaths);

- certain outcomes on the ground are expected but not guaranteed (*e.g.*, when a policy is introduced to pay farmers to maintain grazing at certain livestock density level),

- outcomes on the ground are rather conjectural (for example the result of an increase in the target price for a specific agricultural commodity, such as lamb).

A central purpose of developing methods for valuing public goods and externalities is to reflect real public preferences and provide greater objectivity and precision than can be achieved by policy makers making judgements in their absence. Valuation can also introduce greater transparency in decision making if it reveals the components within a policy equation, the weighting given to different factors and the assumptions underlying the decision. However, this requires the valuation method and its application to be reasonably transparent and comprehensive to an

163|

external audience. Often this is itself a considerable challenge, as the methods used for valuation, the assumptions that they are built on and their deployment in a particular policy question can be obscure to those who have not been closely involved. If used inappropriately, valuation can provide merely technocratic or economic gloss, creating a barrier to effective participation in policy making and provoking suspicion rather than confidence.

It will not and should not remove the political nature of most policy questions. If a valuation exercise suggests that a particular set of rural amenities has a net value which greatly exceeds the cost to a public authority of a programme which appears likely to secure such benefits, then it does not follow that the programme should proceed. Another set of amenities/ and or market goods could generate benefits and many other considerations apply. These include the availability of funds, the administrative convenience of the scheme, the distributional effects in the rural economy, the governments international obligations and overtly political factors, such as the likely reaction of the media and the impact on groups supporting the ruling political party.

There are circumstances where relatively precise valuations are needed, typically where damages need to be calculated and a loss of public amenities translated into a direct cost for which one or more parties are liable. Often it will be appropriate to have administrative guidelines indicating values in broad terms, although individual circumstances vary considerably and damages are commonly determined by legal process. Over time the need to value rural amenities for the purpose of determining damages and compensation and for the evaluation of new projects, such as roads or irrigation schemes, is likely to grow. This is not only because of the growing scarcity of many rural amenities but also because of the development of environmental legislation. In the EU for example, a recent White Paper from the European Commission, sets out the features of a proposed new Directive on environmental liability. This explicitly includes liability for damage to biodiversity on important sites, which would require an approach to valuation, which is workable on a pan-European scale. It would also provide a framework for establishing liability for any environmental damage arising from the growing genetically modified crops, a potentially major issue in many OECD countries. Legislation of this kind will draw the farming community and agro-food industry into realms of environmental policy and judicial process previously more associated with manufacturing industry.

When environmental legislation requires compensation, this does not necessarily take a monetary form. It may oblige a party causing environmental damage to take compensatory action. The destruction of a wetland at a particular site may be permitted to occur only if a new wetland of broadly equivalent value is created or restored elsewhere. In such cases, equivalence will often be judged on the basis of biological value or worth in broader amenity terms but economic valuations will also have a role in some circumstances. The "flexibility mechanisms" under the Kyoto Protocol, which would allow carbon trading, and the offsetting of national obligations by compensatory measures in other countries, such as the planting of forests, indicate that increasingly compensatory measures are likely to be applied at the international as well as national scale. In this context, economic valuation could provide support for policy decisions, especially if specific methods of appraisal for specific types of project were widely accepted internationally. A tool for assisting comparisons and improving consistency of decisions can have merit for those implementing compensatory measures, even if the particular values of a given amenity are contentious.

Where valuation is used for policy appraisal purposes, it must be applied within a matrix that frequently contains a large number of different variations and uncertainties in several dimensions. Often it is difficult to establish precisely what is being measured. For example, if it is proposed to introduce a new policy to encourage the continued management of pastoral area by livestock farmers, at a sustainable grazing pressure, it is helpful to know the value of the resulting landscape in amenity terms. This can be fed into a cost-benefit equation to test whether the policy is worthwhile. Valuation methods can be, and are, applied in such situations. However, several questions arise. Some are generic to valuation methodologies, such as the various forms of CVM that could be used in such an exercise.

These include the appropriate means of handling non-use values, the difficulty of specifying the amenity in a precise way, questions about beneficiaries, etc. Others may be specific to the type of policy being proposed. For example, it is difficult to predict precisely which farmers or land managers will respond to a new incentive, exactly how they will alter the overall management of their farm as well as the practices at which the policy is aimed and how the landscape will change over a period of time. If there are variations in the predicted outcome, how far do these matter, and is their spatial distribution a critical factor? If a policy has a life of five to ten years, and it is uncertain what will succeed it (a not untypical situation), how does this affect the situation?

Given these questions and other uncertainties arising with economic valuation, it is not difficult to explain the relatively limited use of this approach in policy design in the agriculture sector, as noted for the USA in Heimlich's paper. A similar situation probably applies in the EU. It should be noted that the political structure and timetables associated with agricultural and related rural policies may militate against the use of such techniques – more so than in the forestry sector for example. In the EU there has been a substantial growth in the scale of agri-environment policies designed explicitly to generate non-market benefits. In practice, policymakers face considerable constraints on the way in which they implement measures such as Regulation 2078/92 and its successor, the agri-environment Title in the current Rural development Regulation 1257/99. These include:

165|

- The highly political process whereby expenditure targets are determined, both for the EU as a whole and for individual Member States. There may be parallel processes determining the distribution of funds within individual Member States.

- The clear relationship between historic expenditure and the availability of funding for the next budget period, to 2006.

- The relatively short time available between the publication of the Regulation and the deadline for Member States to submit national schemes to the Commission, limited the scope for prior appraisal.

- Specific restraints, such as the need to make available incentive schemes to farmers throughout the agricultural area as far as possible.

These conditions may not be untypical of those applying other OECD member countries. Not do they inhibit the use of valuation techniques in the evaluation of policies that have been put into place. However, the extent to which CVM and other techniques command confidence varies. A recent review of rural policies in England by the government's Performance and Innovation Unit (PIU) is a case in point. This identified a dozen, largely academic, cost-benefit studies of agri-environment schemes, mostly based on CVM techniques. They indicated ratios of net value to public sector expenditure for individual schemes as ranging from about 3:1 to 260:1. The PIU remarked on the difficulties of carrying out such studies and the fact that they do not generate precise estimates of environmental benefits but nonetheless used them as evidence that the schemes provide good value for money (PIU, 1999).

3. The international arena

In the international arena the potential applications of economic valuation are broadly similar to those arising within entities such as the EU or at a national level. Clearly, international comparisons are especially relevant and the audience for a policy appraisal exercise is larger, less likely to share the same underlying assumptions than a national audience. Where trade issues are at stake, the probability of scepticism about certain claims is greater. Potentially the most contentious claims are those concerned with the WTO "amber box" or "blue box", agriculture policies where there is pressure to reduce the level of domestic subsidy but a countervailing argument about the extent to which these policies are required to maintain or enhance non-food benefits.

In these circumstances, widely accepted valuation techniques could contribute to a broader international consensus on the extent of certain environmental and cultural outcomes associated with farming of a particular kind. For example, it may be possible to deepen understanding of the value to a society of a specific crop, such as rice or oranges, and to explain the particular set of attitudes which make up this value in different circumstances, making comparisons with apparently similar crops (or livestock systems) in other countries. This could help to draw out important distinctions such as between traditional and more intensive modern forms of cropping, or between forms of production historically associated with the culture of a region and those introduced recently as economic and commercial conditions changed.

Greater rigour in examining the composition and scale of amenities associated with agriculture, forestry, crafts and other activities could have benefits for both national policy and the progress of international debates. However, it will not offer an equation for eliminating disputes. Similar attributes of a production system may be valued in different ways in different countries despite apparently similar conditions. Comparisons of the absolute value placed on a hillside of moorland grazed by sheep or a terrace of small paddy fields may not be very illuminating. Nor will it necessarily shed light on broadly factual questions, such as the extent to which certain amenities can be produced only by pursuing a particular agricultural practice. Whether or not there is an exclusively "joint relationship" between a form of agricultural production and a set of rural amenities is frequently an issue of particular sensitivity in a WTO context. Valuation methods won't unlock technical questions, such as the feasibility of managing a herb-rich pasture with wild animals, such as rabbits, rather than sheep. Potentially, however, valuation studies could reveal how far a society might prefer either of these two forms of management and the factors underlying preferences expressed in these studies. Is it the quality of the pasture that is valued most highly, or the presence of the sheep?

Exposing such factors could allow a better informed and more structural debate about multifunctional agriculture and generate research into a broader range of rural amenity issues.

However, these remain questions about the inherently local form of many valuation studies, the difficulties of summing the values of entirely different amenities in a single total, the validity of comparing results from OECD countries with those from developing countries, etc.

In this respect, valuation studies belong in a toolbox alongside other sources of data, appraisal systems, economic models, stakeholder consultations and other aids to policymaking. They cannot be utilised out of context without great care; they do not point to uniform policy solutions to agricultural or broader sustainable development questions. They will not demonstrate whether a particular policy is trade distorting. However, they can demonstrate the range and scale of many rural amenities and feed into the continuing and essential refinement of policies as we move from an era of largely incidental to increasingly planned non-market benefits, especially from agriculture.

Chapter 8

Contributions to the Concluding Round Table

1. Hans-Christian Beaumond, European Commission, DG Agriculture

In many countries, there are legal obligations to perform evaluation/valuation. This is in particular the case in the EU when it comes to environmental impact assessments or evaluation of regional and rural development policies. There is thus a basic interest to improve our ability to value environmental goods and rural amenities, as well as evaluate corresponding policies. Attention should be paid to the wide range of valuation/evaluation tools that is available, including cost/benefits analyses, indicators, land planing instruments and the need to improve the understanding of the physical components of rural amenities.

Prior valuation is not a prerequisite to the implementation of policies aiming at rural amenities. Such policies are legitimised by society demand and the democratic process underlying it. On the domestic side, the focus is on cost effectiveness, distribution effects and transparency, as well as on the political process leading to the implementation of such policies. Subsidiarity and devolution are important elements of the European debate, with a view to reaching a wide participation of stakeholders and taking decisions at the relevant political level, from local to EC Institution level.

While some progress has been achieved during recent years on valuation of public goods and externalities, especially in the case of environmental damage or foregone amenities, such valuation, however, remains site specific and resource intensive. In view of the limitations of valuation methods for non-use values, these valuation methods should not replace informed public debates. Further progress in this field would nevertheless be welcome. Experience sharing and stocktaking at international level would help in making such progress and improve the understanding of the various issues at stake. The OECD could be an appropriate forum in that respect. However, the development of international guidelines on valuation would be premature. Further steps in valuation should *inter alia* draw upon developments at the OECD on agri-environmental indicators and rural development indicators. Developments of landscape indicators are of particular interest, as landscape is the relevant unit for many rural amenities and plays thus a pivotal role.

A better linkage with the concepts that are developed at international level is necessary, in particular under the framework of sustainability. In this respect, more consideration should be given to reversibility vs. irreversibility when valuing amenities. Maintaining diversity is also key in this debate. While the main WTO focus is to go for minimally trade distortive policies, welfare considerations need to be comprehensive. The next stage of OECD work on multifunctionality needs to address more specifically how public goods and positive externalities are valued by society and highlight their jointness in production.

2.   Eva Blanco, Head, International Policies Division, Ministry of Agriculture, Spain

In Spain, as a Mediterranean country, we strongly believe in the concept of multifunctional agriculture. That is why we supported its recognition at the 1998 Meeting of the Committee for Agriculture at Ministerial level in the OECD, as well as in other international meetings.

With respect to both the policies related to rural amenities in general and multifunctional agriculture in particular and the ways to assess demand and derive value from them, we would agree that the different demand valuation techniques that have been presented at this workshop could have some use in designing rural policies. It seems that they have been applied for other types of policies, so they can probably be of use in formulating policies for rural amenities as well. Limited resources could be better allocated if the decision makers have demand studies as a help for policy decision making.

However, given the present situation, more research is needed before we can make full use of these demand valuation methods in assessing demand for rural policies that generate or enhance externalities from multifunctional agriculture. From the opinion of the speakers, we can infer that the potential use of these methods is limited and still subject to controversy in the countries that have already used them.

We suggest that a cautious step by step approach is needed. In any case, these methods can be one among the many practical tools to be used in the process of policy decision making, helping to combine societal demands with the need to preserve the environment. Also, it has to be taken into account that some environmental policies can be especially difficult to deal with as far as demand valuation is concerned.

3.   Bruce Bowen, Director, International Branch, Agriculture, Forestry and Fisheries, Australia

There are two key messages that have emerged from this Workshop that have implications for the "multifunctionality debate" in the OECD and the WTO agricultural trade negotiations. First, the Workshop has reminded us of the need for economic rigour in the debate. To date we have seen some wild and exaggerated claims as to the magnitude of the valuation of non-market rural goods. This has included statements like: *"since our government was elected on the basis of a set of policies this implicitly means that our citizens must be willing to pay for current level and form of support provided to farmers"*. From the Australian perspective this sounds to us like claims that *"we have all these rural amenities that can only be provided by support to farmers – we have not measured them but we know they are there"*. This Workshop has clearly shown the folly of accepting these types of statements because the valuation of any non-market good is a non-trivial exercise. We have heard during the Workshop that there are important issues associated with benefit transfer, non-use values and the simultaneous measurement of both positive and negative externalities that need to be taken into account, let alone the choice of the type of methodology to be used in any valuation exercise. These issues need to be addressed in a rigorous way before any valuation of the non-market effects of agriculture can expect to be widely accepted.

The second key message to emerge is that market price support is clearly not the appropriate means to provide payments to farmers for the provision of any non-market benefits that flow from agriculture. The importance of this message should not be underestimated because the OECD's recent Monitoring and Outlook Report still shows that some 70 per cent of support to farmers in OECD countries arises because of market price support policies. Using the EU sugar price as an illustrative example can show the nonsensical use of market price support for this purpose. If for the sake of argument the gap between EU and world prices was attributed to the provision of non-market benefits, this would imply that the recent increase in the gap (as a result of the collapse of world prices) was due to a sharp and sudden increase in rural amenity. This would not make any sense.

An important implication for OECD work on 'multifunctionality' that can be drawn from these messages is that whether or not rural amenities can actually be valued with any precision is to a large degree not that important – especially given the problems associated with valuation issues referred to above. Rather the key issue is the type of policies being used to address the public good and externality aspects of any amenities provided by agriculture. The OECD has a long track record in a number of fields of advocating the use of public policies that are as direct as possible, transparent and non-distorting. Nothing has emerged to-date in this debate to suggest other than the same policy prescription must surely apply equally here.

4. Carmel Cahill, Head of the Policies, Trade and Adjustment Division of the Directorate for Food, Agriculture and Fisheries of the OECD

From the point of view of a policy maker, I would draw the following conclusions from our deliberations of the last two days. Yes, it is feasible to use economic valuation techniques in the valuation of rural amenities including those that belong through joint production relationships to the "multifunctional character of agriculture". Nonetheless, it is clear that in the opinion of the various experts expressed over the last few days use values are considered to be much more amenable to measurement than non-use values. In particular, some scepticism has emerged about contingency valuation methods. In general, there seems to be more confidence in revealed preference methods than in stated preference methods. All practitioners affirm that it is very important to ensure that the choices that people are being asked to make are clear and unambiguous, specific and measurable.

Where do these conclusions lead in the context of multifunctionality? Remember the evolving definition is "the production of multiple commodity and non-commodity outputs that exhibit technical or economic interdependencies on the supply side and on the demand side that some of these non-commodity outputs are externalities exhibiting some characteristics of public goods. The general context is one in which OECD countries are committed to an on-going process of agricultural policy reform and further agricultural trade liberalisation. However, member country positions are somewhat polarised concerning the policy implications, some claiming conflict between reform commitments and the preservation or pursuit of multifunctional outputs while others see strong complementarities.

With specific reference to multifunctionality this suggests three questions:

- Are the valuation methods available to us able to handle questions about marginal changes? We are interested in the values of changes in the supply of non-commodity outputs that may occur as a result of reform. Indeed, do we even know with any confidence what those changes might be?

- Can we adequately incorporate the complementarities or substitution effects that may exist when we try to value simultaneously the demand for a number of linked outputs. There is evidence that adding up demand for individual multifunctional outputs may result in significant over-estimation.

- Given the international context in which the multifunctionality debate is being carried on, what are the prospects for the various valuation methods achieving the degree of credibility and mutual recognition that would be necessary for them to be used in international forums. Whatever the answer to this question, it is clear that the hurdles to be crossed in terms of transparency and accuracy are even greater in any potential use of these methodologies in international negotiations than when their use is confined to domestic policy decisions only.

Given these complexities and the associated risks of policy failure, it seems prudent to explore all possible options – market creation, quasi-market mechanisms such as user fees, voluntary provision, etc., before embarking on difficult valuation exercises. When these possibilities have been exhausted, valuation exercises should be designed as carefully and rigorously as possible to avoid biases. While a lot more development is probably needed before the various demand measurement techniques will be able to be used in an international context, we should not be discouraged. A lot of progress can and should be made in further developing these techniques for use in domestic policy making. The increased transparency and rigour, which this would bring to domestic policy decisions, would certainly help the international debate because, in this as in many domains, efficient and cost-effective domestic policies are also good policies when seen by our international partners.

5.   Kenji Yoshinaga, Director, National Research Institute of Agricultural Economics, Japan

Dr. Yoshinaga underlined that CVM valuation is only measured to evaluate non-use values provided by rural amenities even though it contains several biases. It is also useful to create technical guidelines for CVM application including survey design, scopes and cases for actual application. At present, application of CVM to policy formulation is premature, including international criteria for valuation. However, the discussion on valuation should be continued in the OECD to identify issues to be solved in policy application by examining various cases in Member countries. He also stressed that evaluation of amenity values is an important exercise to create monetary flow from urban to rural areas for rural development. And if values of amenities are properly evaluated, amenity policies are not the only direct targeted ones; indirect rural policies such as employment and tourism are also required to support the management of amenity supply. He noted that the discussion of valuation should cover all amenities that rural areas can provide, and should not be limited by agriculture.

Chapter 9

Conclusions

1. Main results

- Economic valuation can assist in answering real policy questions and generate confidence among stakeholders and public officials regarding the choices they make. Examples were cited where valuation studies had resulted in more or less reliable estimates of amenity values, which had then formed the basis for a policy choice.

- Although they provide important empirical information for policy making, different methods often yield different results for the same problem. Downstream policy decision thus depends on a personal interpretation of the results and assessment of their robustness. Moreover, many studies that are available now were undertaken 5 or 10 years ago, when perhaps the policy questions were different. It was clear from the workshop that policymakers in different fields, countries and settings disagree with respect to the level of credibility they assign to results of valuation studies. In the US, for example, valuation techniques appear to have established a far greater role/legitimacy in policy making than in the EU.

- Some valuations do not meet basic criteria in terms of methodological rigour and coherence, cost, administrative and practical utility, basic data robustness and political legitimacy. It is often difficult, however, for policymakers to recognise good from poor quality valuations

- Valuation studies should be carefully designed and implemented. It is important to pay attention to sample choice, the actual goals of the valuation exercise, and the potential of the technique selected. There is a need for greater clarity about the choices people are being asked to make.

- Nevertheless, even when the methodology may be sound, the fact that many estimates (particularly of non-use values) are based on hypothetical "contingent valuation" surveys, means that the results cannot be taken too literally. There may be large differences between what people say they are willing to pay and what people actually disburse. An example was presented of a willingness to pay mail survey that was followed by an invoice requesting the sum that the respondent had claimed to be willing to pay. While many people paid, the discrepancy was nonetheless large. There are "guidelines" (*e.g.*, National Oceanic and Atmospheric Administration) that exist to assist policymakers in carrying out contingent valuation method studies and that address some of the biases present in the survey results.

• As a result of these uncertainties, participants agreed that summing the values of amenities of different types or in different locations into a single figure is problematic. While data bases targeting benefit transfers are available, transferring results from one region or country to another is also problematic. The implication is that the validity of comparing results from different OECD countries is questionable. Some participants, however, noted that revealed preferences (such as changes in real estate prices or in paid visits to an amenity) provide an economically sound basis for valuation, though these methods could only be used in a limited number of cases.

• Even with simpler revealed preference approaches, important questions remain about the audience and sample – For example, just because people living in distant urban centres do not visit a rural area, does not mean that they assign no value to its amenities. It is important to understand better the nature and characteristics of what rural amenities are if appropriate valuation exercises are to be designed, and policy instruments created.

• There was general agreement among participants that valuation studies belong in a toolbox alongside other sources of data, appraisal systems, economic models, stakeholder consultations and other aids to policymaking. They cannot be utilised out of context; they do not point to uniform policy solutions to agricultural or broader sustainable development questions. They will not demonstrate whether a particular policy is trade distorting. However, they can demonstrate the range and scale of many rural amenities and feed into the continuing and essential refinement of policies as we move from an era of largely incidental to increasingly planned non-market benefits, especially from agriculture.

• A better understanding of this general policy field will also require greater recognition of the importance of property rights, which differ from one country to another, in shaping what governments can and cannot do to support the production of amenities.

• Finally, it is clear that as accountability/transparency and benefit-cost assessment become basic principles of public administration in OECD countries, economic valuation will undoubtedly play an increasingly important role given that it offers a monetary estimate to set against a defined cost. Evaluation units may be needed in public administrations. The challenges for policymakers remain how to assess the reliability of results and how to balance this type of evidence with that from other sources, how to identify the relevant amenities for particular sites, and how to identify the appropriate public whose demand for amenities is to be assessed.

2. Conclusions on future work

From the perspective of TDS's work on rural policy, the workshop highlighted the fact that harnessing the value inherent in natural and cultural amenities remains, essentially, a site specific issue. Moreover, it is the value of the amenity based *policy* in contributing to development of the rural economy that is the key issue, not some objective valuation of the amenity itself. As such, the work programme in this area could focus on developing a typology of policy measures that are intended, directly or indirectly, to maintain or enhance amenities, and identifying the costs of these policies and the range of benefits accruing from them, *e.g.*, what rural amenities contribute to rural economic vitalisation. This work could include studies addressing how rural policies can improve the relationship between amenity preservation and rural economic development, and the factors of social, economic and technological changes that could affect the quality and quantity of amenities in the future.

From the perspective of the OECD's work on multifunctionality and on agri-environmental policy including agri-environmental indicators, the Workshop provided a very useful overview of the state of the art in measuring demand for the non-commodity outputs, including amenities, that are associated with agricultural production. The necessity to simultaneously assess demand for several non-market goods that may be complements or substitutes for one another adds a further degree of complexity to efforts to apply the various techniques. To this extent caution is required in any attempt to apply valuation in estimating demand for the multifunctional characteristics of agriculture. Efforts to develop and refine valuation methodology should, nonetheless, be pursued to bring increased rigour to the policy making process and avoid decisions on government intervention that have no empirical basis whatsoever. But further development is needed before the idea of internationally agreed methodologies could be envisaged.

In any event, a review of the empirical material available on simultaneous demand estimation for non-market outputs that are associated with agriculture will form part of the applied phase of the multifunctionality work to be undertaken in the second half of 2000.

From the perspective of the work on biodiversity, the workshop underscored the need for better understanding the economic characteristics of rural amenities and their relationship to biodiversity conservation. While valuation should not be viewed as the ultimate answer to all biodiversity conservation questions, it is an

177|

integral part of an information toolbox available to policy makers. The wide range of available techniques and the resulting disparities they produce may cause confusion among potential users. To assist OECD policy makers in their decision of when and where to use valuation, the Working Group on Economic Aspects of Biodiversity is in the process of preparing a valuation handbook focused on biodiversity. In issues such as ecosystem services, where the biodiversity and rural amenities agendas potentially overlap, this sort of handbook may be useful for policy makers targeting rural issues.

List of Principal Contributors

1. Experts

David BALDOCK
Deputy Director
Institute for European Environmental Policy
Dean Bradley House
52 Horseferry Road   Tel: +44 171 799 2244
London SW1P 2AG   Fax: +44 171 799 2600
United KingdoM   E-mail: dbaldock@ieeplondon.org.uk

John FOSTER
Centre for the Study of Environmental
Change (CSEC)
Lancaster University   Tel: +44 1524 593 716
Lancaster LA1 4YT   Fax: +44 1524 846 339
United Kingdom   E-mail: j.foster@lancaster.ac.uk

Ralph HEIMLICH
US Department of Agriculture
1800 M Street, NW   Tel: +1202 694 5504
Washington DC 20036-5831   Fax: +1 202 694 5773
United States   E-mail: heimlich@econ.ag.gov

Ian HODGE
University of Cambridge
19, Silver Street   Tel: +44 1223 337 151
Cambridge CB3 9EP   Fax: +44 1223 337 130
United Kingdom   E-mail: idh3@cus.cam.ac.uk

José Manuel LIMA E SANTOS
Instituto Superior de Agronomia
Tapada de Ajuda   Tel: +351 1 360 2072
1399 Lisbon   Fax: +351 1 362 0743
Portugal   E-mail: jlsantos@isa.utl.pt

Douglas MACMILLAN
University of Aberdeen
Aberdeen AB24 5UA
United Kingdom

Tel: +44 0 1224 274 128
Fax: +44 0 1224 273 731
E-mail: d.macmillan@abdn.ac.uk

Ståle NAVRUD
Agricultural University of Norway
P.O Box 5033
N-1432 AS
Norway

Tel: +47 64 948 927
Fax: +47 64 943 012
E-mail: stale.navrud@ios.nlh.no

2.   OECD Contacts

Rural policy

Josef KONVITZ or Andrew DAVIES
Territorial Development Service (TDS)

E-mails: josef.konvitz@oecd.org
            andrew.davies@oecd.org

Multifunctionality/Agriculture policy

Carmel CAHILL
Agriculture Directorate

E-mail: carmel.cahill@oecd.org

Biodiversity/Environment policy

Dan BILLER
Environment Directorate

E-mail: dan.biller@oecd.org